Professional power and social welfare

Radical Social Policy

GENERAL EDITOR

Vic George

Professor of Social Policy and Administration and Social Work University of Kent

Professional power and social welfare

Paul Wilding

Routledge & Kegan Paul
London, Boston and Henley

First published in 1982
by Routledge & Kegan Paul Ltd
39 Store Street,
London WC1E 7DD,
9 Park Street,
Boston, Mass. 02108, USA and
Broadway House,
Newtown Road,
Henley-on-Thames,
Oxon RG9 1EN

Printed in Great Britain by
Redwood Burn Ltd, Trowbridge, Wiltshire

© *Paul Wilding 1982*

No part of this book may be reproduced in any form without permission from the publisher, except for the quotation of brief passages in criticism

ISBN 0 7100 0885 6

CONTENTS

PREFACE

Unless a university teacher has the precious privilege of study leave, writing books is becoming an increasingly difficult and painful task. A project is put aside at the end of one vacation and picked up at the beginning of the next - and that is no way to produce original work. I hope this book does not bear too many of the stigmata of its origins.

Vic George has been all an editor should be - encouraging when things were behind schedule, perceptive in his comments so that even when I would have preferred to ignore them I felt bound to try to take account of them.

My wife and family have lived with the book with great patience and forbearance and I am grateful to them.

Paul Wilding

Introduction

This book is concerned with the power which certain groups of workers exercise in the field of social welfare by virtue of their occupational roles and functions in the welfare state. The groups would all expect or aspire to be recognised as professionals.

Much more has been written about the power and influence of the medical profession than about other professional groups. That will be clear in the chapters that follow. The thesis of the book, however, is that the issue of professional power in social welfare is one which is relevant too in other fields in relation, for example, to social workers, teachers and town planners. Because of this view that there is a unity about the welfare professions they are examined together. Other kinds of professions or would-be professions with important powers in social welfare - accountants and auditors, building society managers, solicitors, architects and surveyors, the police - are not included because their work is clearly rather different.

The book begins with an attempt to locate the professions in the context of society and briefly to consider some of the theories and ideas which have dominated the study of the professions.

Chapter 2 is the core of the book and looks in detail at the nature and extent of professional power in social welfare in a number of different areas - in policy making and administration, in the definition of needs and problems, in resource allocation, in the power exercised over people, and in the power professionals possess to control their area of work.

Chapter 3 discusses the basis of this position of power - the relationship between the professions and the state, the contribution made by the very nature of state welfare, the importance of assumed professional expertise, the legitimacy conferred by the claim for moral veracity and an ethic of service, and the support accruing from general public acceptance of professional activities.

Chapter 4 examines the current critique of the role of the professions in modern society and argues that at its heart lies the issue of professional power. The critique is analysed under seven headings: that the professions have made excessive claims and their achievements have only been modest; that they have been guilty of serious failures of responsibility; that the claim to political neutrality which buttresses their power is a myth; that they trample on people's rights; that the claims to an ideal of service look, on close examination, rather threadbare; that while the professions help some people, they also disable others; and, finally, that the professions are an example of power without accountability.

Chapter 5 attempts to outline a policy for the professions arguing that such a policy is needed because the present relationship of the professions both to society and to their clients is unsatisfactory. It suggests certain ways in which adjustments might be made but concludes that fundamental change in the position of the professions depends on broader social change.

The aim of the book is limited - to raise the question of the position and power of certian professionals in our social welfare system. A general study of this kind can only be exploratory. The issue examined, however, is pervasive and important and merits more consideration than it has so far been given.

1
The professions, society and social welfare

An increase in the number of professional workers has long been recognised as one of the characteristics of industrial society. Goode (1960, p. 902) says: 'An industrialising society is a professionalising society.' In all developed societies there are occupational groups enjoying or asserting certain claims to privilege - autonomy, a monopoly of a particular field of work, the right to control entry to the field of work and a high level of rewards. Because of the size and importance of these groups, defining and characterising what constitutes a profession has been a major sociological industry.

Such a situation raises immediate questions for the student of society. What is a profession? How do professions differ from mere occupations? How do occupations successfully gain admission to the professional heaven? What is the significance of a group of occupations asserting professional attitudes and values? How can we make sense of the professions in the context of an advanced industrial society?

Before proceeding to a consideration of the particular issue of professional power in social welfare it is important to look at some of these more general questions as the backcloth for later discussions. This chapter is therefore devoted to a brief consideration of three general questions about the professions. Firstly, what is a profession? Secondly, how is professional status achieved? Thirdly, what is the significance of the professions?

I WHAT IS A PROFESSION?

No social phenomenon can be understood without reference to the society in which it is set. Society cannot be studied - or at least understood - without reference to social theory. The theory or model of society adopted colours the subsequent interpretation of social phenomena.

Much of the literature on the professions is devoted to the question of what constitutes a profession. In general, the answers produced have not been illuminating. The main reason for this has been that the discussion has been unrelated to social theory. The professions have been studied as if they existed in a vacuum. What most writers have done is to make the seemingly commonsense but limiting assumption that there must be certain characteristics which distinguish professional work from other work and it is these characteristics which make certain occupations into professions. It is an assumption with which the professionals themselves are unlikely to quarrel.

Underlying this assumption, however, is the further assumption that the characteristics of an occupation determine its position and status in society. It is an essentially functionalist perspective though the perspective is seldom made explicit. It assumes that the crucial issue in the evolution of a profession is the fit between its characteristics and the nature and needs of society, and that development is of a biological, evolutionary nature little affected by action on the part of the evolving occupational group.

Even on its own terms the trait approach has been unhelpful. The search for characteristics which discriminate between professions and non-professions has a long history. Flexner (1915), in his famous paper Is Social Work a Profession?, began this search, but it has yielded little in the way of understanding why and how it is that certain occupational groups gain professional status. There is little consistency in the work of those who have pursued this approach. Millerson has reviewed the work of no less than twenty-one authors who tried to define the essential elements of the true profession. He collected twenty-three attributes which were regarded as essential, but no single attribute was accepted by all his twenty-one authors although certain attributes were mentioned again and again (Millerson, 1964). The classic statement of this approach is Greenwood's famous paper Attributes of a Profession, listing five elements which he sees 'as constituting the distinguishing attributes of a profession' (Greenwood, 1965) - systematic theory, community sanction, authority, an ethical code and a professional culture.

The starting point and assumption of the trait approach is that professional work is in some way different. That assumption is, however, seldom regarded as problematic, to be treated with scepticism until proved true. Clearly, demonstrating that professional work is somehow different is a crucial prelude to an examination of its distinguishing attributes and that task is seldom undertaken.

Secondly, the trait approach assumes that somewhere there is a true profession, an archetypal, ideal type accepted by all students and commentators as exuding the very esse of professionalism and, that from it, the key professional traits can be deduced with general agreement. To decide whether or not an aspirant profession is fit and ready to enter the professional fold then becomes a simple task of scoring it on the agreed attributes. The assumption of one true, apostolic profession is, however, highly dubious.

A third objection to the trait approach is that the status of the traits and attributes is seldom clarified. Too often statements of the aspirant group are taken at their face value and assertions of the existence of an ethical code, or systematic theory, or a need for lengthy training are accepted by commentators without investigation or analysis. Students of the professions 'have uncritically accepted the claims and assumptions of the subjects of their study', says McKinlay, 'to an extent which would be unforgiveable in most other areas of sociological enquiry' (McKinlay, 1973, p. 63). The assertion of such characteristics is taken as proof of their existence, as a statement of facts rather than as the plea of interested parties requiring verification. That such assertions are purposive counters in a process of occupational self assertion seldom seems to occur to commentators.

Professional claims need to be regarded critically rather than simply accepted. For example, claims by professions about the need for training need to be looked at in the light of the various functions which training serves. Weber, for example, comments that (Jones in Parry, Rustin and Satyamurti, 1979, p. 73):

> when we hear from all sides the demand for an introduction of regular curricula and special examinations, the reason behind it is, of course, not a suddenly 'awakened thirst for education' but the desire for restricting the supply for

these positions and their monopolization by the owners of educational certificates.

Other professional claims and asserted characteristics need to be examined in the same critical light.

As regards the professions' assertion that they are bound by special ethical codes, Berlant stresses that, as far as medicine is concerned, codes of medical ethics must be seen as organisational tools and resources used by the profession in its bid for a range of privileges and in particular for professional autonomy and monopolization (Berlant, 1975, p. 64). Ethics, he argues, 'can secure group interests as well as patient medical interests by acting as a tool for ordering conduct in a monopolistic direction' (ibid.).

Statements about codes of ethics by the professions or by their critics remain at the level of assertion or allegation. We know very little, in fact, about the supposed service orientation of even the most researched professions. Whether professionals are more infused with an ethic of service than non-professionals who make no such protestations of virtue remains a mystery. If we did the necessary research we might find that the professions and aspirant professions were more motivated by the ideal of service than other occupations. On the other hand, we might find that claims for a service orientation were simply cloaks for the pursuit of self-interested advancement. As Lees suggests, 'it is at least questionable whether professional people are quite the monks growing their own vegetables in selfless pursuit of the public good that their pronouncements and demeanour would often have us believe' (Lees, 1966, p. 17). Till we are better informed we must treat all pleas of moral excellence with scepticism, remembering that occupational groups like individuals, are not in the best position to judge their own rating on a moral continuum.

On the other hand, as Hardcastle has pointed out, 'It is the *ideal* of service or of a "calling", with the practitioner standing above the sordid considerations of the market place, that separates the professions from occupations' (Hardcastle, 1977, p. 14, my emphasis). Reality may be very different from the ideal, but stress on the ideal is not without significance. To be worth making, such a plea must at least contain the appearance of credibility.

Traits and attributes may be characteristics, they may be ideals, they may be assumed as counters in a process of political campaigning. The fact that would-be professions tend to stress similar characteristics may mean no more than that they have studied previous campaigns with diligence and noted the pleas which have proved efficacious in the past. The important point is that any attributes listed by occupational group members must be regarded as assertions until they are proved to be more substantial.

In the writings of those who have sought to isolate the essential attributes of professional work there is little sense that what they are studying are campaign documents prepared in a search for privilege and power or in their justification. The essential reality of professionalism - privilege and power (the very purpose of the claims which are made to particular characteristics) is missing from their work. It is as if the whole issue affected no one except the profession and nothing was at issue except the recognition of work and merit.

The professions exist. If the attempt to isolate the distinguishing characteristics of professional work is unsatisfactory and unconvincing, what is it that distinguishes professions from occupations? Freidson rejects any approach which depends on the nature of the work undertaken and argues that the term profession is to be regarded simply as a description of a certain pattern of occupational control. What is special about a profession, he insists, is that it is 'an occupation which has assumed a dominant position in a division of labour, so that it gains control over the determination of the substance of its own work' (Freidson, 1970b, p. xvii) and, he might have added, of work close enough to its field to be regarded as a potential challenge to its dominance. Johnson argues in a similar vein, 'Those occupations which are associated with peculiarly acute tensions ...', he writes, 'have given rise to a number of institutionalised forms of control, "professionalism" being one. Professionalism then, becomes redefined as a peculiar type of occupational control rather than an expression of the inherent nature of particular occupations' (Johnson, 1972, p. 45).

As with the trait approach, however, the model of society underpinning such a view needs to be made explicit. Implicitly, if not explicitly, Freidson is adopting a conflict or action model, seeing society as an arena in which competing interest groups struggle to secure their own interests. According to such a view, professions are occupations which have come out on top in the struggle.

Professionalism, according to this argument, is a form of occupational control justified by the expert nature of the work involved and buttressed by what Freidson calls the 'persuasive profession of the extraordinary trustworthiness of its members' (Freidson, 1970b, p. xvii). This is what professions want above all - autonomy and control of their own terms of work. To this end are claims for the exclusion of the uninitiated, control of entry, and licensing of members directed. Whether the aim is the independence, prestige, power and prosperity of members of the profession, or the well-being of its clients and the wider society is, of course, an issue for debate. But about the centrality of the claim for occupational control of work there can be no discussion. If this is the nub and kernel of the professional claim, is a profession simply an occupational group which enjoys a particular degree and pattern of control of its own work? The supposed characteristics of professions - service ethic, length of training, and so on can all then be regarded as links in the chain of argument directed to that end, rather than as inherent and inalienable characteristics of the work of particular occupations - in short as attempts at gaining and justifying power and privilege.

Freidson's argument that the term profession is best understood simply as a description of a particular pattern of occupational control is valuable in alerting us to what is clearly a central professional aspiration. It does seem, too, to discriminate effectively between occupations which would generally be accepted as professions, law and medicine for example, and those which merely aspire to such acceptance, social work for example, but have not clearly arrived. It does also embrace the four goals which occupations seeking professional status are usually pursuing: a state enforced monopoly of the task in which they engage; control of entry to the occupational group both in terms of overall numbers and of individual candidates; control of the length and content of training; and, finally, determination of the conditions of work of members of the occupation.

In criticism of Freidson's stress on occupational control it can be argued that his isolation of one characteristic is too specific a way of classifying the key elements in an imprecise term like profession. Becker, for example, argues, that we should regard professions simply as (1971, p. 92)

> those occupations which have been fortunate enough in the politics of today's work world to gain and maintain possession of that honorific title.

He continues:

such definition takes as central that 'profession' is an honorific title, a term of approbation. It recognises that 'profession' is a collective symbol and one that is highly valued. It insists that 'profession' is not a neutral and scientific concept but, rather, what Turner has called a 'folk' concept, a part of the apparatus of the society we study, to be studied by noting how it is used and what role it plays in the operations of that society.

What is a profession? The trait approach is unsatisfactory on two grounds. It is based on an implicit order or consensus model of society and such a model does not help to illuminate social reality. Secondly the trait approach is unsatisfactory even on its own terms, making assumptions which are unjustifiable and falling short of an adequately critical view of statements made by members of professions and would-be professions. The approach which sees professions simply as occupational groups which have secured a dominant position in the division of labour is based on a more realistic action model of society.

The trait approach leaves the evolution of professions as unproblematic. If the achievement of professional status depends on the characteristics of the profession, or the nature of the work, there is little to explain except the precise fit between professional development and particular kinds of society. The view of professions as groups which have secured a dominant position in the division of labour places at the centre of any discussion the question of why and how it is that certain groups attain such dominance.

II HOW IS PROFESSIONAL STATUS ACHIEVED?

The view that it is the characteristics of certain occupations or the nature of their work which bring them the accolade and privileges of professional status sees such status as being granted to certain occupational groups because of their importance to the smooth functioning of the social system. All that then requires examination are the stages and speed of the evolutionary process by which occupational egg grows into gorgeous professional butterfly, and the extent to which there is a pattern which is repeated from group to group - first an occupational association, then a university-based course of training, then occupational control of entry to the occupation, then a professional monopoly - and so on - until full professional status is finally granted by a grateful government on behalf of a delighted and deferential populace.

The flaw in this picture is the absence of any sense of action or struggle by the group involved. The privileges of professional status are seen as granted by society rather than as gained by the profession. There is no sense of action or of politics. There is no examination of how or why government is persuaded of the inherent wisdom of divesting itself of certain elements of power and responsibility in favour of a particular occupational group.

Such a limited view is again attributable to the structural-functional perspective. Such a perspective encourages the assumption that the nature of the work is the all important determinant of status; it is blind to the significance of the class, status and power of the group doing the work. If society is characterised by shared norms and values, and if there is fundamental agreement about social purposes and priorities, then this kind of natural, evolutionary perspective seems entirely reasonable. If, on the other hand, one sees society as characterised by manifest or latent conflict, by diversity of interests, by conflicting goals and purposes, then it becomes important to see the process of professionalisation against this more martial canvas. Occupations and professions are, above all else, interest groups, which is not to say they are motivated solely by self-interest, but rather that they represent certain elements and goals in society which have to be reconciled with other goals and interests. Professional people are also, as Titmuss has pointed out, 'whether they be doctors, social workers or teachers ... pre-eminently people with status problems' (Titmuss, 1968, p. 72). Professional status then becomes the product of action by the occupational group concerned, rather than simply the fruit of certain characteristics or of a particular kind of work.

The struggle for professional status can be interpreted in various ways. Historically, the professions can be regarded as the original achievement of certain aspiring occupational groups in mid-Victorian England 'who sought the highest form in which the middle class could pursue its primary goals of earning a good living, elevating both the moral and intellectual tone of society, and emulating the status of those above one on the social ladder' (Bledstein, 1976, p. 80).

Again, the process of professionalisation can be interpreted more specifically as the process by which, as Larson puts it, 'the occupations that we call professions organised themselves to attain market power'. She continues: 'I see professionalisation as the process by which producers of special services sought to constitute and control a market for their expertise. Because marketable expertise is a crucial element in the structure of modern inequality, professionalisation appears also as a collective assertion of special social status and as a collective process of upward social mobility' (Larson, 1977, p. xvi). The Parrys, too, see professionalisation as 'an occupational strategy of groups who aspire to collective upward social mobility into the solid middle class' (Parry, 1974, p. 182). Professionalism is also a strategy for exercising what Weber called 'social closure'. 'By social closure', Parkin writes, 'Weber means the process by which social collectivities seek to maximise rewards by restricting access to rewards and opportunities to a limited circle of eligibles.' The purpose of singling out the characteristics which distinguish the chosen group, says Weber, 'is always the closure of social and economic opportunities to outsiders' (Parkin, 1974, p. 3).

This view of the process of professionalisation as one of occupational self-assertion, struggle, conflict and, if successful, closure, can be the product of the general perspective that it is more illuminating to take a conflict rather than a consensus approach to society, or it can be the product of a close analysis of the claims and characteristics of the professions, leading to the conclusion that there is nothing particular and distinctive about professional work. For those who adopt this conflict approach the key questions then become 'How does an occupational group gain such a privileged position in society?' or 'Why does the state grant a range of privileges and accept a loss of power to this particular occupational group?' Without doubt the nature of the work, the degree of expertise and trust involved and its importance in society are all significant. So, too, are other factors - the power of the group, the compatibility of its interests with the interests of powerful groups in society, the measure of support which the group has from wider public opinion.

The professions will argue that the privileges which they seek, which are the prizes of a recognised professionalism, are not privileges but logical conditions necessary for the fulfilment of their work. Whatever the relationship between the nature of professional work and the working conditions necessary for its pursuit, however, it is undeniable that the conditions which the professions seek to achieve are of positive material benefit to themselves and, in less exalted groups, could easily be mistaken for pure self-interest. How, for example, should we regard control of entry to a profession and the insistence that those who wish to practise its work should be licensed? Should we regard these as an attempt to protect clients from the inferior wares of unscrupulous and unlicensed practitioners, or should we regard them as an attempt to secure a monopoly and create and maintain an economically advantageous scarcity? Most writers have seen licensing as somehow 'necessary' to protect society and have ignored the clear and obvious benefits to the occupational group involved and the important fact that demands for licensing usually originate from the would-be profession rather than from the public whose interests are supposedly in jeopardy. Licensing, Berlant argues, in relation to the medical profession in the USA, is not the product of non-professionals concerned to protect the public interest but is introduced at the request of professional groups seeking legal privileges (Berlant, 1975, p. 129). Roth argues the same point in his assertion that in licensing the crucial factor is 'the political power of the occupational group which seeks this type of protection' (Roth, 1974, p. 21). Why should the state grant privileges to particular occupational groups? In part, the granting of autonomy, control of entry and other powers is the product of the feeling that political control of certain activities is undesirable, that such control should be separated from political authority and handed back to the experts. Underlying this view is the belief that certain forms of action are apolitical and value free, and that there is consensus in society between society, users and professionals, about how the activities should be organised and carried on.

On the other hand, it may be that the state recognises that political and administrative control would be impossible given the particular expert nature of the activity. Traditional methods of control would be both ineffective in providing protection for consumers and inhibiting for the professionals. State encouragement for the development of professional organisation and the granting of powers and privileges to that end can then be regarded as the product of an attempt at securing the best protection for the public. Heidenheimer has suggested a variation on this theme of necessary delegation of powers to professions pointing out that in the USA the creation of 'specialist jurisdictions through which organised professional bodies exercise a mixture of de jure and de facto control over vital policies affecting their sectors' was a way of 'circumventing inept or corrupt State and local administrative agencies' (Heidenheimer, 1973, p. 331). Certainly, professional self-regulation often predates the development of the infrastructure of central and local government necessary to external regulation of the professions.

The state may prefer, then, to hand over control to the occupational group itself on certain conditions - which is where the 'characteristics' of the professions come in. For it is only acceptable and trustworthy groups with a measure of organisation and structure which get such favoured treatment. Part of the pluralist view of the world is that there are many sources and kinds of power in society of which political power is only one. Recognition of the professions implies the acceptance of the power of expertise as something beyond or above politics.

Another possible view is that the privileges of professions represent a kind of truce situation between powerful blocs, a mechanism for accommodating the powerful and potentially conflicting interests of the state and powerful occupational groups. The state 'needs' the profession to perform important social functions; the profession 'needs' the state to enforce licensing and monopoly. Both need each other, and the granting of professional status can be regarded as a practical method of fitting certain powerful occupational interests into a democratic society, a process of expert, occupational incorporation. Before granting such privileges, however, the state needs assurances that they will not be abused and the service orientation and ethical code, and perhaps the class background and the values of the profession, provide the kind of reassurance - real or tokenistic - which the state requires to legitimate such abdication of responsibility.

At the heart of the explanations is the issue of the connection between professions and would-be professions and the state. The existence of a profession with its various rights and powers represents a measure of abdication or sharing of power by the state whether on grounds of the principle that some areas of expert decision making should be left to the experts, or on grounds of expediency (that some areas will be better controlled and regulated by leaving them to the expert occupational group involved), or on grounds of sheer necessity (that the only way to accommodate powerful groups of providers of key services is to have power sharing). The connection between the profession, or would-be profession, and the state then becomes crucial to the process of professionalisation. The connection may be multi-dimensional, rooted in the value of the work to the well-being of society or in the social connections of the occupation or its leaders with dominant social groups, or the connection between the values of the profession and values dominant in society.

What produces the privileges of professional status is a profession—state alliance. 'The foundation of medicine's control over its work', writes Freidson, 'is ... clearly political in character, involving the aid of the state in establishing and maintaining the profession's pre-eminence' (Freidson, 1970b, p. 23). 'A profession', Illich writes, 'like a priesthood, holds power by a concession from an élite whose interests it props up' (1978, p. 50). To secure such support, members of the occupation have to prove their trustworthiness and reliability in relation to their expertise and to dominant social values. Professionals have to show that, by their social standing or through their work, they help to support and maintain and strengthen the existing economic, social and political order. 'A compatible constellation of interests', as Berlant puts it (1975, p. 306), has to exist between professions seeking social closure and powerful social groups. Various factors in the relationship can contribute to such a compatibility of concerns but it has to exist.

The issues to be explored if the question as to how professional status is achieved is to be answered, are twofold. Firstly, there is the whole area of the nature and extent of the occupational group's power and influence which enable it to climb the ladder to professional status. Then there is the issue of why the state is prepared to give away substantial elements of control over particular occupational groups.

III WHAT IS THE SIGNIFICANCE OF THE PROFESSIONS?

What is the significance of the professions and what is their role and function in society? A number of writers have speculated in a relaxed, post-prandial kind of way suggesting points which may or may not be true, but which are not susceptible to testing of any kind, and which are unrelated to any theory of society. Durkheim, for example, saw the professions as an influence for social order and social solidarity, as bonding forces filling a vital gap between the family and the state, helping to link men to the social system (1966, p. 49).

In their pioneering and seminal work Carr-Saunders and Wilson waxed eloquent about professional associations as stabilising elements in society for 'They engender modes of life, habits of thought and standards of judgement which render them centres of resistance to crude forces which threaten steady and peaceful evolution.... It is largely due to them and to other similar centres of resistance that the older civilisations stand firm' (1933, p. 497). Talcott Parsons stresses the 'strategic significance in our society' of a set of occupational groups which are not, either in their own opinion or by and large in the public estimation, devoted mainly to the 'goal of their own profit, but rather in some sense to service' (Halmos, 1970, p. 193).

Paul Halmos argues in similar vein, accepting that the professions may not be all that they say they are, but insisting that the moral aspirations they assert are a social fact of some importance. 'It is the nature of "aspirations"', he suggests, 'that their advance imagery exerts a pull on a reluctant and hesitant present' (1973b, p. 8). The direction of such professional 'pull' is towards the introduction of more collectivist and other-regarding considerations into the 'social functioning of individuals', and in weakening 'the _laissez faire_ licence of a free enterprise, the _rapacity_ of penal justice, the _harshness_ of educational discipline and the _mercenariness_ of "marketable" doctoring' (Halmos, 1970, pp. 57-60).

The process of professionalisation, Halmos argues, 'is the widest single avenue along which moral change in our Western industrial communities is being guided today, or will be guided during the coming decades' (ibid.). He sees the professions, and particularly the personal service professions, as providing a kind of moral leadership in society and, because of their power and influence, he believes that 'their interpretation of social realities and their formulation of social standards will continue to remain the authoritative and obvious guide of social reappraisal and social change for all, and especially for the professions in the impersonal services' (ibid.).

These ideas are interesting and suggestive but they do not

greatly help to an understanding of the basic role, functions and significance of the professions. Here the two models of society which I used earlier help to open up broader issues. An evolutionary, consensus model of society leads to the view that the professions have evolved because of their fit with the nature of our kind of society and that they have come to prominence because they express in action certain central social values - for example, society's concern for the health or education or well-being of its members.

The development of professions is clearly connected with the nature of modern society. Daniel Bell's 'The Coming of Post Industrial Society' has as one of its central themes the idea that power follows knowledge (Bell, 1973). Robert Lane argues that in the knowledgeable society experts and expertise inevitably become more important. 'It appears to me', he writes, 'that the political domain is shrinking and the knowledge domain is growing, in terms of criteria for decisions, kinds of counsel sought, evidence adduced, and nature of the "rationality" employed' (1966, p. 658). Such a change leads to the growth and consolidation of groups of experts around particular areas of knowledge of social importance.

Another relevant characteristic of the knowledgeable society is structural differentiation - the increasingly sharp division of labour which characterises mature industrial society. A range of activities previously undertaken by the family, the community or by informal groupings within it, becomes the province of experts. The narrowing of functions of the family or, more correctly, their increased sharing with specially created social institutions, is an example of this. It is of the nature of the industrial system to lead to the division of labour and the professions express and further this specialisation.

A further important relevant characteristics of industrial society is the collectivist, welfare ethic of governments of virtually all political complexions. Professions become an important part of the apparatus of welfare collectivism. The expansion of the role of the state in welfare has been a factor of major importance in the expansion and development of the welfare professions. It has led to the growth of some old professions - medicine for example - and the expansion of occupations - social work for example - with strong professional aspirations. A commitment to welfare by government means a need for professionals - to advise on the organisation of services, to manage, man and mediate services, to decide questions of eligibility and need, to individualise justice, to raise standards of health and child care. The professions claim to have expertise which can be used to solve or alleviate situations agreed to be social problems and the claim is accepted. The professions' good faith is accepted too, and so they are given power to tackle the problems in the ways they think best.

According to this view, the professions can be seen as expressing society's concern and response in the face of situations agreed to need some kind of collective action - for example, the diswelfares inherent in economic and social development, the problems of socialisation in a complex society.

A conflict model of society will locate the professions in the context of the conflict which is regarded as the dominant characteristic of society, whether manifest or latent. The professions may well be seen from this perspective as in Shaw's phrase 'a conspiracy against the laity'. Such a view fits best with what might be styled a pluralist conflict model, in which the conflict is seen as between fundamentally ad hoc groups such as occupational, regional, sex groups, or between professions and bureaucracies. The professions are then one warring group among many, seeking to advance their own interests and further their own collective mobility and this can only be done at the expense of the laity. As Adam Smith put it a century and a half before Shaw, 'People of the same trade seldom meet together even for merriment and diversion, but the conversation ends in a conspiracy against the public or in some contrivance to raise prices' (Lieberman, 1970, p. 135).

The flaw in this view is that it does not take into account the important fact that the more significant powers and privileges of the professions are granted by governments. Government has to be persuaded of the rightness or expediency of, for example, granting an occupational group monopolistic power. What is granted can, in theory at least, be taken back. Why governments grant power and privileges to professions depends on a range of facts - the social connexions of the profession and its leaders, the social value of the profession's work, the power of the profession, its degree of popular support and so on. But it is government which grants the powers which make the conspiracy possible.

According to this view, professions are occupational groups which have been taken over by the state or have forged an alliance with it. This leads to another interpretation of the professions from what could be regarded as a Marxist conflict perspective. This view would see the professions as instruments of state power - in our society as lackeys of the capitalist state or, as Marx described economists, as 'hired prize-fighters' of the bourgeoisie (Miliband, 1977, p. 59). The key force in the development of the professions, according to this theory, is not professional self-interest but the interests of dominant social groups. If one accepts the idea of the unity of the state in capitalist society, that all the elements of the state work as one for the reproduction of capital and labour and the preservation of a particular and inequitable social order, then the professions are a not unimportant part of the state machine. They operate essentially as a force for social control in its broadest sense, seeking, for example, to alleviate some of the health-denying impact of industrial capitalism through the provision of state medicine, to socialise the next generation to an ethic of competition, individualism and self-help, to locate the causes of delinquency and deviance safely within the individual rather than in the economic and social system.

The great service which professionals render to government is that they both express social concern and exalt expert solutions to social problems at the expense of political solutions. 'As social problems become the concern of professionals', Galper writes, 'the professionals become involved in a problem solving domain where problems and their solutions are seen as technical rather than as structural or political' (1975, p. 92). The rise of the professional estate is both a product of the view that social problems are amenable to solution by technical, administrative, expert manipulation, and gives that view added support and credibility. Such a witness and its profoundly conservative implications is of great benefit to governments. It is both a contributing cause and a happy beneficiary of the end of ideology view of the world. It is no accident that Halmos (1965) gives the first chapter of 'The Faith of the Counsellors' the title The Discrediting of Political Solutions. That is the tide on which the professions reach harbour and it is a development which they help to legitimate. Professionals stand for the solution of problems within the existing social system, they are the technicians and tacticians of piecemeal social engineering rather than the strategic planners of social change.

Professions gain power and influence as experts who are

technically and politically useful to governments. Their use, and the granting of power to them, is legitimated by the technocratic rationality which is part of the ideology of advanced industrial society. They, in turn, by the standing and the status which accrue to them as the trusted experts of governments, legitimate the use of experts to solve problems which at other times and from other perspectives might be regarded as political. The sphere of the expert grows, the legitimate sphere of political activity narrows. Technocratic rationality becomes in Habermas's words 'a specific form of unacknowledged political domination' (Esland, 1976, p. 34), more difficult to challenge than political judgments because of its seeming scientific and expert base.

The professions therefore fulfil three functions in advanced capitalist society. They stand as an expression of state concern for private troubles which have been accepted as public issues. Secondly, their expertise legitimates state action. As Scull (1975, p. 219) has pointed out, 'Elites in such (modern) societies over about the past century and a half have increasingly sought to rationalise and legitimate their control of all sorts of deviant and troublesome elements by consigning them to the ministrations of experts.' Expertise cloaks and legitimises the exercise of state power. Thirdly, the welfare professions provide a rich source of desirable jobs in the public and private sectors for members of élite and middle-class groups where such groups can enjoy varying degrees of power, privilege and freedom in their work and, through their efforts, help to maintain the system which supports them in varying degrees of elegance.

The significance attributed to the professions depends on the model of society which is adopted. But whatever the model, there can be no dispute about the power the professions wield. That, perhaps, is the most significant aspect of the professional estate. Surprisingly, it has been little examined. Such neglect is part of a broader problem. 'I have been struck', Wrong writes in his study 'Power: Its Forms, Bases and Uses' (1979, p. 52),"by the fact that one finds little or no discussion of authority based on specialised knowledge or skill in most analyses by social scientists of the various forms of influence, power and authority.' There have been studies of the power of particular professions in relation to particular issues but there has been little attempt to look in a general way at the power the professions wield in modern society. This is interesting because as long ago as 1939 Talcott Parsons noted that 'many of the most important features of our society are to a considerable extent dependent on the smooth functioning of the professions' (1954, p. 34). Titmuss made the point more specifically in 1964 (p. 196) arguing that 'In the modern world, the professions are increasingly becoming the arbiters of our welfare fate; they are the key holders to equality of outcome; they help to determine the pattern of redistribution in social policy.' It is the nature, extent and significance of that power that needs to be examined in more detail because it is a crucial element in state welfare services.

2
The nature and extent of professional power

The nature and extent of the power of professionals in social welfare varies from profession to profession, from service to service, from situation to situation. What is clear, however, is that in many areas professionals have wide-ranging powers. The discussion in this chapter examines the nature and extent of professional power under five different headings: power in policy making and administration; power to define needs and problems; power in resource allocation; power over people; and power to control the area of work.

Any discussion of the nature and extent of professional power is going to tend to be dominated by discussion of the medical profession. Its power is more obvious and better documented than that of any other professional group. The thesis of this chapter, however, is that the medical profession should be seen as an example of a more general characteristic of welfare states. The discussion therefore draws for examples on other professions and semi-professions and seeks to advance the argument on a broad front.

I POWER IN POLICY MAKING

The most obvious example of professional power in policy making is the role of the medical profession in relation to health policy. 'The history of the British health service', says Klein (1973b, p. 7) 'is the history of political power, Ministers, Civil Servants, Parliament, accommodating itself to professional power.' All the major changes in the organisation of health services this century - 1911, 1948 and 1974 - bear witness to the power of the medical profession both to determine the terms of discussion and to ensure that any changes take full account of the profession's demands and interests.

Gill's study of the role of the British Medical Association in the formulation of the National Health Insurance scheme of 1911 is a story of the success of the medical profession in gaining all its central demands. In the end, says Gill, 'General Practitioners entered the service practically on their own terms' (Cox and Mead, 1975, p. 160) with the BMA's six cardinal points all in large measure accepted by the government.

It was the same story in 1946 when the National Health Service was created. The story of events between the Brown Plan of 1943 and the Act of 1946 is what Willcocks (1967, p. 103) describes as 'a process of erosion' - erosion of government plans in the fact of pressure from the medical profession. To compare the terms of the Act of 1946 with the 1943 plans is to get some idea of just how successful professional pressure had been. The idea of a salaried service had gone, so had the proposal for local government control, so had a tidy, unified administrative structure, so had a regional organisation embracing teaching hospitals.

The story, of course, does not end in 1946 when the National Health Service Bill became law. Eckstein has described how much of the National Health Service Amendment Act (1949) was negotiated rather than discussed between the Minister and the profession. The same was true of the National Health Service Regulations finalised during 1947. 'What the B.M.A. had been denied during the drafting of the N.H.S. Bill', says Eckstein, 'it got immediately after its enactment.... What was granted, in effect, was the right to argue a case rather than merely to present it, and an assurance that agreement with the profession would be earnestly sought, not just that its views would be taken into consideration' (1960, pp. 101-2).

The influence of the views of the medical profession during the discussions on the reorganisation of the NHS between 1968 and 1974 was by all accounts profound. The views of the profession, in fact, determined the terms of the debate and the parameters of the possible by excluding certain proposals from the start - in particular local government control and any change in the position of the general practitioner. 'To a large extent', say Brown and his colleagues (1975, p. 101), 'the structure of the reorganised N.H.S. was modelled to the desires of the medical profession.'

Do other professions have a comparably commanding position in policy making? 'There seems to be a widespread public belief', Manzer comments (1970, p. 45), 'that doctors know what is the best organisation for medicine but there is no such belief that teachers know what is the best organisation for education.' Teachers lack the status of doctors, they are regarded with less deference, their work may be important but it does not deal with issues of life and death. Their expertise is less mysterious and less obvious, they have not been as successful as doctors in asserting their special role as generalised wise men vis-a-vis anything remotely to do with education.

Having made these reservations, the role of the teaching profession in educational policy making is central. Kogan describes the teachers' associations as 'only a wafer away from the Local Authority Associations in consultative status'. Though the Local Authority Associations have a stronger role in formal decision making, 'teachers' associations are party to many of the most important decisions. They do not see every official promulgation in draft but certainly they are consulted about most of those which affect the interests of their members or the running of the education system in general' (Kogan, 1975, p. 102). The role of the profession in the educational policy making process is certainly important. There is an accepted right to give evidence to any official committee on education. The profession has successfully opposed the proposal for auxiliary teachers in the classroom. It scored a significant professional victory when it persuaded Edward Short, when he was Secretary of State for Education, to make teaching an all-trained profession by ceasing to allow unqualified staff to teach. The National Union of Teachers would argue that it has successfully pressed the importance of primary education on the policy makers of the Department of Education and Science. It has also been a force for the abolition of selection for secondary education - encouraging the then Labour Government to come out decisively for the abolition of selection in 1965 and clearing the way for it to do so, pressing Local Authorities to abolish selection and leading the opposition to Mrs Thatcher's refusal to approve schemes for comprehensive reorganisation in the years after 1970 (ibid., pp. 113-14).

The DES is, however, clearly less tender towards the susceptibilities of the teachers than is the Department of Health and Social Security towards the doctors. In health there are certain policy issues which de facto are ruled out of discussion - salaries for GPs, for example, or local authority control of the Health Service. Policy has to be made around these reserved areas. Non-cooperation by the doctors or even withdrawal from the Health Service remains a threat with sufficient force, in political terms if not in reality, to keep the DHSS extremely sensitive to the demands of the profession. Such sources of strength are not so readily available to the teachers.

What of the influence of social workers on policy making? Two pieces of recent legislation where social work influence has been very important are the Children and Young Persons Act 1969 and the Local Authority Social Services Act 1970.

The two controversial White Papers - 'The Child, the Family and the Young Offender' (1965) and 'Children in Trouble' (1968) show the triumph of social work definitions of the problem of delinquency. The assumption writ large in the White Papers is that social workers are the experts on these issues; they know the answers and therefore the decision about the nature of the 'treatment' required is one for them - the experts, rather than for lay magistrates. The 1969 Children and Young Persons Act, which was the legislative outcome of 'Children in Trouble', marks a significant transfer of power from magistrates to the professionals.

It is a tribute to the power and influence of social workers that the Seebohm Committee was set up in 1965 to review the organisation and responsibilities of the personal social services. The composition of the Committee is again a comment on the success of the social work world in convincing the relevant authorities that the issues were such that social work representatives should dominate the Committee. The non-social work members were less organised, less convinced of what should be done and were therefore easily carried along in the rush for social services departments (Hall, 1976).

The system of town planning set up in 1947 gave town planners a powerful position. The new system, says Peter Hall (1973, p. 373),

> held that the values of society should be interpreted and guided by professional planners, monitored and controlled in the last resort by democratically accountable political power, but with a great deal of freedom not merely in day to day administration but also in the formulation of basic policies.

Planning was a new field; it was a complex field. Even if the planner did not positively make the final decisions he did decide which policy options were placed on the agenda and so set the terms of the discussion by his political masters. 'In the end', as Eversley (1973, p. 343) puts it, 'decisions depend on the presentation of policy options by the planner'.

Evidence of the power and influence of the welfare professions in policy making and administration is plentiful. It is less easy to pick out the significance of that power for the development of services, but three suggestions can be made about it. Firstly, and most importantly, professional influence means that in many issues the decisions made serve professional interests rather than the public interest. A second indictment of professional influence is that it leads to services organised according to professional skills and ideas rather than according to client need. Thirdly, it means that certain elements and interests within the professions are able to dominate decision making because of their greater prestige and status.

It is not difficult to find evidence for the thesis that professional interests rather than the 'public' interest have powerfully affected the development of health provision. For example, the continued absence of a unified health service providing a coordinated pattern of care is a major flaw in the organisation of health care. One of the aims of reorganisation in 1974 was to create an integrated service and failure to achieve this aim is directly attributable to professional insistence that the general practitioner's position as an independent contractor must be preserved and so remains as a major obstacle to full integration.

Another area, where the public interest in securing effective health service planning has been blocked by professional interest in securing that no action takes place without professional approval, is in the arrangements for the operation of District Management Teams. The profession secured that each Team should be made up of the District Administrator, the District Finance Officer, the District Nursing Officer, an elected consultant, the District Community Physician and a GP, all with a right of veto over team decisions. This victory weakens the whole structure of the service. Things can only get done with the agreement of the medical profession. The profession has, in effect, a power of veto over decisions affecting management.

Another much criticised characteristic of the NHS which we owe to the medical profession is its highly bureaucratic nature. To listen to the complaints of the profession one could easily assume that it was the victim of some kind of disabling political and bureaucratic conspiracy designed to enmesh the profession in administration. The converse is the truth. As Klein has pointed out:

> To think of the system as a kind of bureaucratic conspiracy against the NHS is to miss the point. Committees have proliferated largely because the medical profession insisted on being concerned with the decision making process; in turn the other professions and Trade Unions represented in the NHS have pressed for similar rights. (1976)

A further area where professional interests and the public interest have had to seek a compromise solution is over the geographical distribution of general practitioners. Maldistribution was an acute problem in 1946 but the profession fought hard to secure freedom of movement for its members - and largely succeeded. The basic pattern of distribution of GPs remains very similar now to the situation thirty years ago. The gentle negative direction and the succulent carrots, which was all the profession would allow the ministry by way of a policy, have achieved relatively little (Butler et al., 1973).

While teachers have played a much less significant role in the development of education policy that the role played by doctors in the development of health services, they are still, however, open to the charge that their concern has been with professional interests rather than with the public interest. In his study of the chequered history of the proposals by the Plowden Committee for positive discrimination through educational priority areas, Banting pays close attention to the role of the National Union of Teachers. His verdict is that 'Opposition from the N.U.T. was sufficient to reshape important parts of the E.P.A. proposal' (Banting, 1979, p. 153). The issues which aroused the fiercest opposition were those proposals which seemed to threaten teachers' professional status. The Union was extremely cool towards any suggestion of pressure from the Department of Education and Science for increased parental participation and opposed vigorously Halsey's proposal in 'Educational Priority' for nursery centres - a sort of hybrid play group cum nursery school. 'The idea of parental involvement', Banting writes, 'was still suspect and the Union disliked the parent-run play groups movement, on which Halsey's proposal was partly based. The N.U.T. insisted that nursery education be provided in the professionally run educational system' (1979, p. 135) - which has meant that it has not been provided.

An early draft of what became DES Circular 2/73 on Nursery Education had urged Local Education Authorities to 'take all possible steps to encourage parents to play a more active role' and had included a paragraph of detailed suggestions from Halsey's report but, after objections from the teachers' unions, these recommendations were progressively watered down until the final circular simply asked Local Education Authorities to 'extend opportunities for collaboration' and dropped the specific suggestions entirely (Banting, 1979, pp. 135-6). The teachers feared the loss of professional status threatened by such a degree of parental participation and fought to restrict it in spite of the considerable evidence of its educational benefits.

Shortly after the publication of the Seebohm Report calling for the reorganisation of personal social services into social services departments, Sinfield questioned the basis of the social work pressure for such a development. 'A citizen reading the report', he commented, 'might indeed conclude that it had more to do with the work satisfaction and career structure of the professional social worker than it had to do with his own needs or rights in the modern welfare state' (Sinfield, 1969, p. 2). The Report was conceived and written from the standpoint of aspirant professional social workers rather than from the viewpoint of actual or potential clients. The interests of the public received less attention than professional needs. My argument is that this is frequently the pattern of professional influence in policy making.

A second criticism of professional power and influence in policy making and administration is that it leads to services organised according to professional skills and ideas rather than according to client needs, to provider- rather than consumer-oriented services. In the early years of the NHS Titmuss alerted his readers to the new problem 'that the hospital may tend increasingly to be run in the interests of those working in and for the hospital rather than in the interests of the patients' (1963, p. 122). Crossman's dislike of large District General Hospitals was the product of the view that they had been developed for professional reasons. 'The case for the big new district hospitals', he argued, 'is almost entirely a consultants' case.' The convenience of the consultant was given very high priority, the convenience of the patient and the family who wished to visit him a very low priority' (1976, pp. 269-70). R.G.S.

Brown goes so far as to describe the division of responsibility between health authorities and social service authorities as 'the most serious impediment to the rational development of priority services' (1979, p. 218). This division is directly attributable to professional power and influence. The first Green Paper on the reorganisation of the Health Service stressed the potential advantages of the integration of health and personal social services under local government (HMSO, 1968a). So did the Royal Commission on Local Government (HMSO, 1969b, para. 359 et seq). Involvement with local authorities has always, however, been quite unacceptable to doctors both as 'a fundamental threat to the status of the medical profession in the NHS, and as an undesirable introduction of political forces into a "non-political" sphere of activity' (Levitt, 1976, p. 208). Social workers are equally apprehensive of the effects of any integration with a doctor-dominated health service so the problem cannot be solved in that way. The result is separate services organised around professional skills - medicine and social work - which makes the provision of integrated care for certain vulnerable groups - the elderly, the mentally ill, the mentally handicapped, the chronic sick - more difficult. Services are organised around professional skills rather than around client needs - because of professional needs.

In social services departments the thrust of development since their creation has been along the lines of professional provision of services rather than of a nurturing of and building on existing patterns of kin and neighbourhood services. Instead of seeing their role as being to supplement an already existing infra-structure of services, the new departments' aim was - or seemed - much more to supplant, than to supplement, what already existed. Michael Bayley makes this point very forcibly in his critique of the White Paper 'Better Services for the Mentally Handicapped' (1971) where family and neighbouring services are seen as supplementing official services. In fact, Bayley, argues, the only realistic way to regard official services is as supplementing the more important family and neighbourhood systems of care (1973, chs 18 and 19). All the studies done by social scientists of the care of special needs groups show the almost marginal importance of public and professional services, and yet professional dominance in the organisation of services secures the institutionalisation of professional ideas in patterns of service organisation and development.

Professional control of the area of work is a major factor in the coordination problems which afflict the organisation of services to particular needs groups. Looked at from the other direction, the seriousness of problems of coordination is evidence of professional influence over the development of services. Because professionals control, and seek to control, their own work territory, no one can ensure that an integrated, coordinated package of services is delivered to the consumer. Each professional, concerned say with the mentally or physically handicapped, tends to see his role as crucial and assumes that someone else, somewhere else, is doing any necessary coordination (Jaehnig, 1979, p. 6). Lack of coordination is the price to be paid for professional control of professional work and the organisation of services according to provider rather than consumer needs and the weaknesses of management which are the inevitable corollary. Professionals cannot unfortunately be regarded either as expert or disinterested advocates of particular forms of service organisation.

The third criticism which can be made of professionals and particularly of the nature and extent of professional interest in the NHS, is that it means that certain particular professional elements and interests dominate decision making leading to biased unbalanced development. Hospital medicine dominates the NHS at the expense of primary medical care because, according to professional ideologies, hospitals are where real medicine is practised. Within hospitals, the emphasis has been on the development of high technology medicine rather than on the development of caring services. Horrobin sees this as in some measure due to the dominance of consultants in prestigious specialisms in policy making. They think only in terms of hospitals as places for short term treatment and curing because that is why their patients are in hospital. They are blind to the need, and the very real role, for small hospitals as places for long term caring. They have therefore pressed ahead with the closure of small local cottage hospitals, failing to realise that people need hospitalisation for very different reasons (Horrobin, 1978, p. 24).

What is striking is the high technology bias of modern medicine in the face of the fact that almost half of all hospital patients are psychiatric or geriatric patients who stand to gain little from the developments on which modern medicine has concentrated. As Dr Mahler, Director General of the World Health Organisation, commented a few years ago 'the major - and most expensive - part of medical technology as applied today appears to be more for the satisfaction of the health professionals than for the benefit of the consumers of health care (Abel Smith, 1976, p. 221).

It is clear that the influence of the medical profession has been a powerful force in perpetuating the disadvantaged position of the Cinderella sections of the NHS. Consultants in the traditionally prestigious specialisms dominate, implicitly and explicitly fixing standards and priorities and setting a value on different kinds of medical practice.

Given that one in six of the population is now 'elderly', and that the number of people aged over seventy-five is increasing rapidly, the fact that a quarter of the medical schools in London have no permanent staff concerned with geriatrics suggests a strange bias among medical concerns. 'It is hard to escape the conclusion' says Bosanquet (1978, p. 146), 'that in the name of "clinical freedom" a certain pattern of medical education is being maintained which fits very oddly against the pattern of need in the community. It would appear to reflect mainly the vested interests of particular groups of professionals.'

Another specific example of the effect on patients and would-be patients of the dominance of certain sections of the medical profession over other less prestigious and so less powerful elements, is the contrast between the resources devoted in the NHS to tonsillectomies and the provision of hearing aids to the elderly. One hundred thousand children per year have their tonsils removed (of whom it is estimated that less than a quarter actually benefit) because paediatrics and surgery are prestigious activities (Williamson and Danaher, 1978, p. 43). The provision of hearing aids is a highly effective service in remedying deafness, and the resulting social isolation, but it is a low status and medically uninteresting activity. Probably one million elderly people could benefit from such provision, but their needs have low priority (Cooper, 1975, p. 97).

Social workers have effectively dominated discussion about the development of personal social services. Till very recently, for example, money devoted to training was almost entirely devoted to full-time courses for social workers. The possible contribution of other kinds of staff and their need for training has been little discussed because social workers have persuaded policy makers that their's is, in some way, the vital role and the use of different kinds of workers amounts to dilution. The result has been to narrow thinking about the development of social care services.

The aim of this section has been to argue that the power of the professions in policy making and administration is important and, in three respects at least, is problematic. At times it serves professional interests rather than the public interest, it leads to the development of services organised around professional skills rather than client needs, it leads to the biased development of services because the dominant groups in particular professions are able to dominate policy.

The argument is not that professions cannot contribute positively to policy making. Clearly they can and do. 'The role of professional groups in improving the quality and range of provision', says Adrian Webb (Hall et al., 1975, p. 91), 'is an important one and it can be vital to the development of newly established services.' Rather the argument has been that professional influence can be problematic, serving professional interests rather than the public interest. A service with a substantial body of prestigious professionals among its staff possesses a built-in pressure group for its development, albeit along professional lines. A service without such a group - for example housing - lacks an important force for its development. But professional concerns are narrow and partial and not immune from self interest.

II POWER TO DEFINE NEEDS AND PROBLEMS

Fundamental to the power of the professions in policy making and administration is an acceptance of their right to define needs and problems. It underpins their power and provides a necessary legitimation for its exercise. This section seeks to explore this issue.

T.H. Marshall sees as a crucial element in the professional's claim to a particular status that he or she has the responsibility of giving the client what he needs rather than what he wants (1963, p. 156). That is, the profession defines the client's problem for him rather than accepts his prior definition. Goode also argues for the salience of this particular element in professional work. In his consideration of whether or not librarianship can be regarded as a genuine profession, Goode cites as decisive the fact that librarians respond to the expressed desires of their clients rather than to their needs as defined by the librarians themselves. Librarians cannot, therefore, claim the status of professionals because, as Goode sees it, a service orientation in terms of professionally defined needs is an essential element in the status of a profession (Vollmer and Mills, 1966). Reflecting on the professional's position, Haug and Sussman describe as 'the core of his autonomy, the right to define the nature of the client's problem' (1969-70, p. 159).

Professional definitions of needs and problems are a powerful influence on policy. Freidson, for example, talks of the modern state 'whose notions of public good are guided largely by professions' (1970, p. 352). If this is indeed the case, it is a major source of professional power. Until recently, for example, the medical profession has defined health in terms of health services. It is only in the last few years that the profession has come to look more closely at diet, exercise and environment as central to the maintenance of health. Medical definitions of health as something maintained by the medical profession and medical services have been the dominant ones in modern medicine. They have dominated thinking about the provision of health care and ensured the dominance of the medical profession.

Another interesting example of how professional definitions of problems have carried the day is the way the medical profession has successfully defined the main problem of the NHS as one of shortage of resources. The profession has done little actively to campaign for more resources, but it has successfully defined the problem of the NHS in these terms. The medical profession therefore escapes all blame for the shortcomings of the service and virtually removes from the agenda all examination of how existing resources are used - or misused. Governments, the Treasury, the DHSS become the villains to be blamed. The central problem of clinical freedom and resource use remains safely off the agenda.

A further area of social policy where professional definitions of need have been important for policy and for the happiness and well-being of many people is housing. In Britain we have moved away from reliance on market definitions of fitness and unfitness towards a definition to be made as a matter of professional judgment on the basis of certain criteria laid down by statute. Definition of fitness and unfitness cannot be objective. Ultimately it is a matter of judgment. Housing policy makers have accepted professional definitions rather than the definitions of those seeking housing. A mass of research evidence now exists showing the gap between professional and consumer definitions. The work of Norman Dennis (1970, 1972), Jon Gower Davies

(1972), and Robert McKie (1971) show that the criteria on which people judge the acceptability of housing, and the things they complain about, are often quite different from the issues on which the professionals make their judgments. Yet the power which the professional has in defining a house as unfit is immense. For years professional definitions were virtually unchallenged.

The power of the planners to define needs and problems is, however, not confined to the field of housing. As Walsh has pointed out, 'it is the planners, rather than the politicians or community groups, who are thinking about the directions in which the metropolis should grow, about desirable standards for education, housing and community services, and about the future of urban society' (Cox, 1976, p. 137).

An example of the power of social workers to define problems and secure acceptance of their definition which was mentioned earlier is the 1969 Children and Young Persons Act. The Act rests on a particular definition of deviance and a particular set of beliefs about appropriate action for dealing with it. How did these professional definitions of the problem gain acceptance in the Home Office? Bottoms argues that developments in social work were directly influential. He suggests that the publication of the Seebohm Report (and the social work ethos and values of which it was so redolent) and the creation of the new British Association of Social Workers 'probably crucially assisted the institutionalization of professional social work concepts within the Home Office at the relevant time' (Bottoms, 1974, p. 333). Whatever the reason, a particular definition of a problem was adopted by the policy makers and became enshrined in statute, a definition which was acceptable to few outside the charmed circles of the social work world, the Children's Department of the Home Office and certain tender-minded Fabians.

In what ways if any is the power of professionals to define needs and problems problematic? Firstly there is the narrowness of the professional vision, a narrowness which has a number of differing dimensions. Because professionals in social welfare tend to deal only with individuals, they define and conceptualise problems in individual rather than in structural terms, a bias which often limits their work to amelioration or providing palliatives.

Again, professionals show a tendency to define problems in ways which seem to bring them with surprising frequency within the legitimate bounds of their professional concerns -

alcoholism and addiction as diseases, pregnancy as illness, delinquency as maladjustment, the needs of the disabled as being for services rather than cash or work - and so on. Ills become illnesses, grief becomes depression. Such narrowness of vision is a dubious basis for policy making. Too often professional recipes for policy making amount to nothing more than a plea for more doctors, more social workers, more teachers - more people like us, the people defining the problem in 'professional' terms.

An example of this narrow professional approach can be drawn from a reinterpretation of a point made by Vincente Navarro in his discussion of the bourgeois bias of the medical research establishment, though what he interprets in class terms could also be interpreted in professional terms. Navarro sees the priority given to research on the supposed individual causation of disease to the exclusion of other factors as an example of this bias. It could also be interpreted as an example of professionals concerning themselves with aspects of health on which they might hope to have some effect, as a narrowly professional definition of the problem. For example, research on heart disease has focused on diet, exercise and genetic inheritance, matters within the widening purview of the medical profession. The evidence that work satisfaction is a crucial element in longevity and the avoidance of heart disease has not been followed up. That is outside the areas of life which even the most optimistic medical imperialist could hope to influence and yet evidence suggests it may be crucial (Navarro, 1978, pp. 118-19).

It is the narrow vision of the medical profession which has led to the focus of health services on disease rather than on health. The doctor spends his time seeing sick individuals. He finds it difficult to rise above such preoccupations and accept or act upon the fact that 'the greatest potential for improving health is through changes in what people do, and do not do, to and for themselves' (Fuchs, 1972, p. 229). A narrow vision and great influence in policy making leads to misdirection of services.

This professional myopia can also induce a blindness to the needs of particular groups. The most obvious example of this is the way in which many members of the medical profession continue to define the problem of mental handicap in medical terms. The medical profession dominates hospital provision for this group and this has meant a neglect of the educational and occupational needs of patients and a lamentable failure to develop adequate services (National Development Group for the Mentally Handicapped, 1978). Definition of the problem as medical has inhibited the active involvement of other professional groups who might better have met the needs of the handicapped.

Another example of the narrowness of professional definitions of problems is the way the Town and County Planning Association has defined the urban problems. 'It has viewed the main problem', write McKay and Cox, 'as overcrowding and urban sprawl which would best be solved by planned dispersal to new and growth towns. As a result, the TCPA has been preoccupied with the growth sector of urban change, rather than with the social problems characteristic of inner city decline' - which are now recognised as the major urban planning problems (McKay and Cox, 1979, pp. 242-1). The professional view of what planning was all about blinded planners to major aspects of the urban problem and led to a policy vacuum.

Because of the narrowness of perspective, professional definitions often ignore or bypass moral and political issues. 'By the very acceptance of a specific behaviour as an illness', Zola (1972-3, p. 500) suggests, 'and the definition of illness as an undesirable state, the issue becomes not whether to deal with a particular problem, but how and <u>when</u>.' Ideas about the nature of delinquency and faith in their competence to deal with it led social workers to ignore certain important issues of liberty and justice in the 1969 Children and Young Persons Act. They could only see the individual's need for help, not the need for justice to be seen to be done and for safeguards against abuse. Their preoccupations were with the individual and this blinded them to the context of their work.

In addition to the various problems raised under the narrowness of vision which characterises professional definition of needs and problems there is the problem that professional definitions represent what Peter Berger describes as 'cognitive imperialism'. Berger's argument is a simple one. As regards meaning, 'every "inhabitant" of a world has an immediate access to it which is superior to that of any "non inhabitant"' (Berger, 1977, p. 142). If the professionals' definitions carry the day, then an essential element in the situation - the 'inhabitant's' understanding, may be neglected or ignored. Without such understanding, the 'problem' is unlikely to be fully grasped or effectively tackled. Professional definitions may be right or wrong, but they are usually imposed rather than agreed definitions and that is a material flaw.

One of the best illustrations of Berger's argument is R.A. Scott's study 'The Making of Blind Men'. The essence of Scott's thesis is that 'Blind men are not born, they are made' (1969, p. 121) and they are made by the professionals. 'When those who have been screened into blindness agencies enter them', he argues, 'they may not be able to see at all, or they may have serious difficulties with their vision. When they have been rehabilitated, they are all blind men. They have learned the attitudes and behaviour patterns that professional blindness makers believe blind people should have (ibid., p. 119). The blind person is rewarded for adopting his rehabilitators' definition of his situation and punished when he clings to his own self-conception. 'Gradually, over time, the behaviour of blind men comes to correspond with the assumptions and beliefs that blindness workers hold about blindness' (ibid.).

Elsewhere, Scott contrasts the American situation with the situation which prevails in Sweden. There, the blind organised themselves and took over the major blindness organisations. No sighted person was allowed to hold executive office. Observation of the Swedish situation led Scott to the judgment that 'professional ideologies about blindness ... are distinctly different from the ones that prevail in countries in which services for the blind are in the hands of seeing people ... what is distinctive about the Swedish program is the absence of an ideology that requires the blind person to undergo intensive personality restructuring or basic changes in self' (Scott, 1970, p. 282). Little attention is paid in Sweden to the issue of psychological adjustment. Financial resources go either to the blind in the form of direct financial aid or to research centres which work to develop specific practical aids asked for by the blind themselves.

For our purposes, the point which Scott is making is that professional definitions of problems may well be very different from the ideas of those actually living the situation. It is professional definitions, however, which determine, in many cases, the pattern and direction of services and as gatekeepers to those services the professionals are able to impose particular constructions of social reality on those who seek to use them. The definitions of the inhabitants of the world of blindness may be superior but they are easily and often overruled.

In defining needs and problems professions tend both to define problems in such a way that they come within the accepted bounds of professional expertise and to extend the boundaries of assumed professional skill to embrace them. 'The medical profession', Everett Hughes argues, 'is not content merely to define the terms of medical practice. It also tries to define for all of us the very nature of health and disease' (1958, p. 79). Such a task is outside medical expertise but is the offspring of a sense of expertness and the cognitive imperialism to which Berger draws attention.

The power of the professionals to define needs and problems is considerable. It is a power which is problematic because of the narrowness of professional vision and the occupational risks of cognitive imperialism. In one further way the power of professionals in this area is important. Because of their assumed expertise and impartiality the professions became, in Adler and Asquith's words, 'probably the main carriers of welfare ideologies' (1979, p. 6). Their definitions help shape public beliefs and attitudes as well as the terms in which governments view issues. The professional influence on government is therefore two fold. It is both direct and indirect, mediated through close profession-government links and through government responsiveness to public opinion - which in turn is substantially shaped by the professions.

III POWER IN RESOURCE ALLOCATION

There are various approaches to the study of professional power and influence in resource allocation. It can be examined at the level of broad planning decisions about resource allocation by central and local government. At this level, it is more a matter of influence than power. Alternatively, it can be explored at the organisational level where professionals make decisions about resource use. Another starting place is the point at which professionals meet individual clients and service users both in dramatic life-and-death situations such as the allocation of kidney machines or selection for heart transplants, and in more routine decisions which are nevertheless important for individuals' welfare. Another approach, which is the one adopted here, is to look briefly at the extent of professional power in resource allocation and then to analyse its effects.

Professional power in resource use is substantial and is often exercised with few political or bureaucratic controls. The way in which the hospital sector has increased its share of NHS resources since 1948 is a tribute to the power and influence of the medical profession at the level of central government planning. Crossman refers on numerous occasions in his diaries and elsewhere to the power of hospital consultants over resources. When he tried to shift resources towards services for the mentally handicapped after the Ely scandal he 'received a memo from the Chief Medical Officer telling me I could not possibly put to the Regional Hospital Boards the need to shift priorities to the subnormal area without upsetting the consultants and having a blow up in the medical service' (Crossman, 1977, p. 455). Crossman's well-known lecture 'A Politician's View of Health Service Planning' takes up this argument in general terms and argues that the NHS is a consultant-dominated service for it is the consultants who decide the direction of development of the service through their power over the allocation of resources (Crossman, 1972, pp. 21-6). Heller argues that a switch of resources to primary care and services for Cinderella groups '<u>cannot</u> take place given the present power structure within the Health Service. The switch will be resisted by those powerful factions that have already distorted the system into its present shape' (Heller, 1978, p. 95).

Some years ago the Department of Health and Social Security explained the balance of power in resource use to the House of Commons Expenditure Committee. 'The Health and Personal Social Services', the Department stated, 'have always operated on the basis that doctors and other professional providers of services have individual professional freedom to do what they consider to be right for their patients. Thus in each individual doctor-patient situation, it is the doctor who decides on the appropriate objective and appropriate priority. This is not to say that the Department cannot impose overall constraints or influence behaviour, for example by the imposition of charges, but it is important to note that the existence of clinical freedom substantially reduces the ability of the central authorities to determine objectives and priorities and to control individual facets of expenditure' (Klein, 1974, p. 32).

In the NHS, as Brown points out, it is doctors' decisions which 'effectively commit most of a health authority's resources' (1979, p. 210). David Owen estimated that in 1975 the average general practitioner controlled resources worth £25,000 per year - some £15,000 of this being the cost of the prescriptions he writes. The average hospital doctor and his nursing colleagues controlled resources worth some £100,000 per year and each consultant in 1975 controlled the spending of about £500,000 (Owen, 1976, pp. 81-4).

The writing of prescriptions is the most obvious way in which the general practitioner controls resources. He also, of course, uses resources when he refers patients for tests and examinations and when he makes requests on behalf of his patients for services such as home helps or rehousing. The doctor's control over resources is however much more wide ranging than this. Doctors regulate access to their own services through appointment systems, surgery hours, and through the attitudes they inculcate and the powers they allow to their receptionists. Similarly, the general practitioner determines the quality and quantity of the service he provides - that is of the resources he uses - through the length of time he devotes to his patients, the number of home visits he makes, whether or not he encourages patients to return to the surgery to report progress, whether he allows his receptionist to deal with repeat prescriptions.

The extent of the general practitioner's power to control the service he offers, the extent to which he underuses, misuses, or overuses his most expensive resource - himself - is virtually untrammelled. His patients are unlikely to complain formally about strict rationing of the service or its massive dilution, and the terms of their contracts leave general practitioners safely insulated from external intervention except in cases of gross neglect. The general practitioner's control over the resources he commands is a major element in the power of the medical profession over the resources of the NHS.

The doctors 'clinical freedom' of course, gives him the right to prescribe whatever treatment he considers appropriate with minimal checks. He has, in effect, a blank cheque on the system, though it may not always be honoured. It is a valuable principle and one for which the medical profession has rightly fought hard. It is an ideal, but in an unideal world it conflicts with the harsh facts of life. Quite simply, the notion of 'clinical freedom' assumes unlimited resources which the medical profession then has absolute power to deploy as it thinks best. Unfortunately, resources are not unlimited and one man's freedom in that situation becomes another man's restriction.

As far as education is concerned, Byrne's conclusion from her study of three very different Local Education Authorities was that 'in all three LEA's, the Education Departments enjoyed reasonable autonomy over the establishment of their own priorities for development' (Byrne, 1974, p. 309).

And the priorities of the Education Department were essentially the priorities of the Chief Education Officer - professional priorities in resource use.

Little is known about resource use within schools, partly because that is a matter for head teachers who operate only within very broad policy guidelines. What is clear, however, is that the head can distribute resources - in this case largely staffing resources - in ways which can substantially affect the lives of the children in the school. He can institute smaller teaching groups for less able children or a wider range of options for the sixth forms; the more experienced and better qualified staff can be allocated to the abler children, the less experienced and less qualified staff to the less able children, for example - and it is almost impossible for anyone to challenge his decisions.

Byrne's conclusion in her study 'The Rationale of Resource Allocation' is to stress the influence and power of individuals to commit resources as against the power of plans. 'The individual influence of key personnel (chief education officers, heads, principals)', she writes, 'is often more decisive than any prearranged planning' (Byrne, 1976, p. 9). From our perspective, what she is stressing is the power of professionals over resources.

Like doctors, social workers have a considerable measure of freedom in how they use the resource of their own time. Because social workers find certain kinds of work more rewarding, and because it fits more easily with particular notions of the social work task, they spend more time and attention - and so more resources - on some kinds of work than on others. Work with families and children is regarded as more worthwhile than work with the elderly and handicapped or with people with material difficulties (Rees, 1978, p. 141).

The decisions of professional staff can also commit very substantial amounts of departmental resources. The interpretation which social workers place upon a care order may commit many thousands of pounds of resources over many years, or virtually no resources at all. Similarly, the priority given to an application for a place in an old people's home has important resource implications - and the decision is one made by the professionals.

The most obvious financial resource which social workers control is the payments which they can make under Section I of the Children and Young Person Act 1963. The sums spent under this provision are small - £5m per year in the late

1970s - but the payment is often critical to the survival and well-being of a family. The social worker's power over the disbursement of such money is very great. As Hill and Laing (1979, p. 38) put it when discussing the procedures, 'If social workers say "No", that is normally the end of the matter ... in no sense can they be said to be processing "applications" for help from clients who must be given formal decisions'. Jackson and Valencia's (1979, p. 98) conclusion was very similar - that basic grade social workers were left to make decisions about applications for material aid with very little control or guidance. 'We know of no social work department', they concluded, 'which publishes details of the criteria by which it gives financial aid (even where such criteria exist) and none where a formal appeals system operates' (ibid.).

Cochrane points out how, when new types of operation or treatment to which considerable prestige is attached were introduced, there was, in the past, a marked tendency for all teaching hospitals and many others to feel they should undertake such work regardless of the number of cases likely to require treatment in their particular hospital. Such a proliferation, Cochrane argues, is not to the benefit of the patient who would gain from as few centres as possible to give medical staff the maximum amount of experience. It is also a prodigal use of precious resources, for example, for a large number of London hospitals to be undertaking open heart surgery. In 1967, forty-five hospitals were doing operations to insert permanent pace-makers in patients needing such heart treatment. Ten of these hospitals, however, did only one such operation in that year (Cochrane, 1972, pp. 82-3). With the greater resource constraints of recent years, such extreme examples of prodigal resource use are probably rarer, but as indications of the power of the professionals in resource allocation they retain their validity.

What are the effects of this substantial measure of professional power, influence and autonomy in resource allocation? There are four which will be examined here.

The most obvious effect of professional power in resource allocation is that, whatever the supposed priorities of the political policy makers, the professionals can substantially determine the way in which the service actually operates. Control over resource use means that publicly determined priorities can be negated. Where official priorities are unpopular with the professions - as were those of 'Priorities For Health and Personal Social Services' (HMSO, 1976) - they will have little effect on the actual pattern of service provision. The medical profession was not enthusiastic about giving greater priority to certain special needs groups - and they managed to make sure that government intentions bore little fruit.

A recent plea for 'A Development Agency for the NHS' reports an interesting case of such 'local provider' or professional power over resources. The original plan for a particular District General Hospital set aside ninety beds for geriatric care. By the time the hospital opened a decade and more later, when the numbers of over seventy-fives had increased very considerably, the surgeon/consultant lobby on the hospital's medical executive committee had reduced the geriatric allocation of beds to thirty. Eventually, as a result of intervention by the Regional Health Authority sixty beds were set aside for geriatric cases (Tether, 1979). But professional power had still cut the allocation by one third.

A second effect of professional control over resources is that services can be deployed for professional convenience rather than in line with client need. We saw earlier the great power which the general practitioner wields over the resources he commands. The crucial issue is how those resources are used and there is considerable evidence in support of the view that recent trends and developments in how resources are used in general practice, have been for the benefit and convenience of the doctor rather than of his patients - appointment systems, changes in surgery opening hours, the development of health centres, the use of deputising services. Professional control of resources can become a professionally focused and self-centred control with little or no opportunity to challenge how it is exercised.

Thirdly, professional control over resources negates planning and management. If so much depends on the decisions of individual professionals, then there can be little generalised planning of resource distribution and no easy re-ordering of expenditure patterns. 'The NHS tacitly accepted', writes Cooper, 'that the activities of doctors were outside of managerial control. Management has decided what resources should be made available at each level, whilst doctors have been left free to decide their best deployment' (Cooper, 1975, p. 108). The 'Priorities' document stressed the need for a critical scrutiny of the use of resources in general and acute hospital and maternity services if future growth in resources was to be limited and if resources were to be switched to the chronic sector. How was this critical scrutiny to be carried out? The DHSS was able to do no more than register an aspiration. 'It is hoped', it concludes, 'that the professions will continue to examine the implications of different types of treatment for resource use' (HMSO, 1976, para. 23). In the end, the professionals decide the crucial questions about length of hospitalisation and what they will spend on drugs - and administrators can do little to enforce their desires or decisions.

A fourth effect is that such professional control usurps the appropriate sphere of political decision making. The justification for professional control of resources is that the decisions to be made are essentially expert and technical and can only be made by those with specialised knowledge. That may or may not be true, but clearly in some of the examples cited no expertise was involved. The implications of such decisions may well significantly affect the distribution of goods, services and opportunities for individuals, groups and classes.

A number of writers for example, have argued that town planning is much more than simply a technical activity because of its important role in the distribution of spatial resources. Planners, however, have considerable power and influence over the distribution of resources in the spatial structure - through the way their decisions effect changes in the location of jobs and housing, in the value of property rights and the price of resources to the consumer.

The emphasis in planning orthodoxy on the dispersal of population from decaying inner cities to peripheral estates, new towns and growth towns has had very real distributional consequences, serving in Pahl's words 'to draw apart the more skilled workers, who have been able to consolidate and establish their new position in the new and expanding industries, from those with low or no skills who have put up with low pay as well as poor housing and access to other facilities' (1970, p. 239). The power of the planners lay in the idea, unchallenged until the 1970s, that such decisions were technical rather than political.

Planning decisions can affect property rights and so the capital value of the assets of owners or landlords. Roads built for reasons of unchallengeable technical judgment can destroy property completely, can reduce its value by destroying amenity, or can enhance its value by increasing acceptability and accessibility. What the planners are doing is, in effect if not in intention, to reduce or enhance property values. They are distributing resources.

Such decisions about the location of new estates, the course of new roads, the location of greenbelts and new schools are, of course, taken by duly constituted political bodies - planning committees, the full local council, the Minister - but the fact that such decisions are seen in technical rather than political terms means their distributional implications cannot sensibly be questioned by lay politicians and so are seldom debated. Technical decisions are for experts, which gives the relevant profession power which cannot lightly or easily be challenged. In 'Public Participation and Planners' Blight', for example, Norman Dennis notes how local councillors hardly figure in his study because their role was so insignificant - until final decisions were made. The planners' view was that 'Not only did the councillors know nothing ... they were not entitled to know anything' (1972, p. 238).

Different professionals have different types and degrees of power over resources. The power of the head teacher for example is restricted to the use of the resources granted to him by his LEA - though he may use his influence to increase them. The planner, on the other hand, has no power, only influence. Planners do not unilaterally make decisions about resource use - as do doctors and head teachers - but have to convince the appropriate committee of the wisdom of their recommendations. Doctors have influence over governmental decisions about the broad pattern of resource use and virtually unlimited power over the actual use of resources for individual patients.

Some professionals have to have power over resources if they are to do their job, and they may well be the only people with the requisite knowledge to make the relevant decisions. The three crucial and critical questions are firstly, how extensive are those powers? Secondly, do they extend beyond the limits of what is required for the individual professional to do his job? Thirdly, there is the question of the effects of such professional control on the use to which resources are put.

IV POWER OVER PEOPLE

Power in policy making, in the definition of needs and problems, and in resource allocation is, of course, power over people in that it affects substantially who gets what in the way of services. Such decisions may mean death or life. Many professionals, however, also wield more direct and immediate powers over people. They are granted by society in view of the expertise and the moral reliability which the professionals are assumed to possess. Such power is inherent in much professional work. In any society, for example, the doctor's expertise gives him a measure of power and influence over those who seek his advice. In modern society, however, with a sizeable public welfare system, the issues become more significant. More and more professionals work in public organisations. This increases their command over resources and, if their organisations are monopolies, over their clients since there is then little freedom of choice for the consumer. The reorganisation of personal social services into unitary social services departments, for example, makes it virtually impossible for a client to invoke the help of one social worker in dealing with another. Even if the organisations in which they work are not monopolies, the very fact of working in an organisation increases the power of the worker. 'Increasingly professionals are buttressed in their authority relations', Marie Haug writes, 'by *virtue* of their location in complex organisation settings.... Professional power at the point of service delivery is power over *clients*. Location of practice in bureaucratic systems puts professionals in touch with authority structures which can be used to enforce their decision' (1975, p. 201).

Some such powers are directly and explicitly conferred by statute, others are granted less explicitly. For example, the doctor in the NHS has freedom to cross patients off his list if he does not wish to continue to treat them for whatever reason. He can also refuse to accept patients on to his list without giving any reason. There is good evidence that in some areas doctors will not take on patients who have left neighbouring practices (Foster, 1979, p. 493). Such power is a useful way of quietening complaint and bringing the awkward patient to reason. What is, on the face of it, a reasonable and sensible right for the doctor can easily be turned into arbitrary power. Such a right clearly buttresses the doctor's power to deal with his practice and his patients as he thinks best without too much reference to his patients' wishes or opinions.

The power which professionals wield over people is power over the sick, deviant and delinquent of various kinds and over those who, for socially defined purposes, come within the purview of the social welfare system. Clearly someone has to make decisions on issues such as compulsory admission to mental hospitals, and on whether delinquents and criminals should, or should not, be committed to penal institutions of various kinds and for how long. Historically, such decisions have generally been regarded as matters of law to be judged by the courts, or by a man or woman's fellow citizens on the basis of custom, common sense, human experience or instinct. More recently, the notion has been propagated and accepted that there is an expertise in these matters, that common sense, judgment, and experience of the world are no longer adequate or sufficient qualifications. The result has been the transfer of considerable power from the courts to certain groups of professional workers - doctors, psychiatrists, probation officers and social workers. The powers are often very great and the procedural safeguards which surround them are normally extremely limited.

A treatment ideology, propagated by professionals and serving the promotion of their interests whether incidentally or by design, is at the heart of this increase in professional power over people. Where a condition - physical, mental or social - is defined as sickness, then the person afflicted is no longer responsible for his condition or his cure. The initiative necessarily and rightly passes to those who have the knowledge to deal with him. 'Where illness', says Freidson (1970, p. 244), 'is the ubiquitous label for deviance in an age, the profession (or professions) that is custodian of the label is ascendant.' The underlying assumption of the medical model of deviance is that the patient is incompetent to judge what is needed and must therefore put himself passively in the hands of professionals to be re-socialised or cured.

The Royal Commission on the Law Relating to Mental Illness and Mental Deficiency which reported in 1957 asserted in its opening paragraphs that 'disorders of the mind are illnesses which need medical treatment' (HMSO, 1957, para. 5). Illness is the responsibility of doctors. They decide who is ill, who needs treatment, of what kind and for how long. This assertion by the Royal Commission led logically to the recommendation to end the role of the courts in compulsory admissions and to an acceptance of the power of members of the medical profession to make orders for such admissions.

The medical profession did not seek such a role. The

evidence presented to the Royal Commission by the various medical associations favoured the retention of judicial intervention for longer term patients. The role was thrust upon it by the Commission and subsequently by the Mental Health Act 1959. With her customary prescience, Barbara Wootton suggested in the House of Lords, in the debate on the Bill which became the 1959 Act, that the temptation to exalt the medical profession 'does sometimes place doctors in an invidious position, and sometimes possibly lays them open to the exercise of powers which the public would regard as arbitrary in other connections' (Bean, 1980). But she was a voice crying in a noble wilderness.

The 1959 Act provided essentially for three types of compulsory admissions to mental hospitals - under Section 29 for observation for up to seventy-two hours, under Section 25 for observation for up to twenty-eight days and under Section 26 for admission for up to one year. For admissions under Section 29 only one medical recommendation is required and the doctor does not have to have any special qualifications or experience in psychiatry. Two medical recommendations are required for orders under Sections 25 and 26 - under Section 25 one of the doctors should have special competence in the field of mental health and under Section 26 both doctors have to state the psychiatric condition of the patient and that no other form of action is appropriate.

The clinical assessments of the medical recommendations do not have to be substantiated. There is no right of appeal for any patient prior to admission and there is no right of access to a Mental Health Review Tribunal for patients admitted under Sections 29 or 25. The Mental Health Act also stops short of defining the key terms on which its operation depends - terms such as 'mental illness', 'mental disorder' or 'in the patient's own interest' - so an enormous amount of discretion is left to the doctors and the social workers who operate the compulsory powers. The Act, too, says nothing about how the doctor is to operate, how he is to gather the necessary information and so on. He is free to do what in his professional judgment is necessary. There are other elements in the compulsory admission procedure which leave the power of the professionals virtually untrammelled. The doctor does not have to inform the patient of his legal rights under the Act, or even the section of the Act under which he is to be admitted. Faulty procedures do not invalidate the admission. The doctor does not have to give reasons for his decision. The whole admission procedure can take place in secret (Bean, 1975, p. 229). To all intents and purposes there is no machinery for reviewing the original decision to admit a patient compulsorily. The jurisdiction of the Review Tribunal is limited to deciding an applicant's fitness for discharge at the time of the review. The appropriateness of the original decision to detain is not open to challenge. That decision cannot be questioned. The power of the doctors and social workers is absolute.

Changes proposed in the recent 'Review of the Mental Health Act 1959' (HMSO, 1978a) will not substantially alter the situation. There is no suggestion of the introduction of a right of appeal prior to admission. Patients could still be detained on the recommendation of one doctor and one social worker. A patient entering hospital voluntarily could still be detained on a long term order with no right of appeal prior to this change of status.

Not only do professionals possess power to detain the mentally ill; there is also power to treat. Without consent, treatment of an informal patient cannot be undertaken. 'Detained patients are, however, compulsorily detained for treatment and while treatment is more readily administered with the consent and cooperation of the patient, the question of consent has already been dealt with legally by arranging compulsory detention' (RCP, 1979, para. 30). To meet the concern about the conditions under which hazardous or irreversible treatment is given to compulsory patients the White Paper suggested a second opinion in certain restricted circumstances (HMSO, 1978a, para. 6.25). The Royal College of Psychiatrists rejected such an assault on clinical freedom and expressed itself as ready to accept a second opinion as mandatory in only two forms of treatment, psychosurgery and Electro-convulsive therapy for a patient refusing to give consent (HMSO, 1978a, para. 34). Currently, however, psychiatrists still possess what Hoggett calls 'this unrivalled power over other human beings (for who can deny that it is that, when major and irreversible surgery can be imposed on a compulsory patient with no independent supervision?)' (1976, p. 57).

The other most significant transfer of power from the courts to professional workers is that which was enacted in the Children and Young Persons Act 1969. Under that Act social workers, including probation officers, have three major functions: in relation to the decision as to whether or not a child should be brought to court; in relation to the preparation of reports on the child and his background; and in the actual provision of treatment. Under the Act the criterion for public intervention is, in general, not the child's or young person's offence but their need. Assessment of need is a matter for professional judgment. 'Need, used as a noun', Illich (1977, pp. 22-3) argues generally, 'became the fodder on which professions were fattened into dominance.'

The power of the social worker is seen at its greatest if the court makes a Care Order committing the child to the care of the local authority. Then 'the discretion of the social worker in England is subject to few checks' (Parsloe, 1976, p. 79). How social workers make decisions in such cases is not known but the decisions are made behind closed doors and are subject to few, if any, checks or safeguards. The decision may be to send the child home or to commit him to a secure institution. John Rea Price talks of the child 'who is consigned to the interminable tunnel of the care order, under which, without any right to independent review short of a formal application to the court for revocation of the order, he can be placed - at the Local Authority's whim - with foster parents, in secure accommodation, a children's home, in lodging or at home on trial' (1978, p. 205).

There are three issues underlying the controversy about the division of powers between court and social workers in the 1969 Act. Firstly, there is the issue of whether social workers - or for that matter anyone else - have in fact the expertise to make the kind of decisions required by the Act. The Act assumes the existence of a corpus of knowledge which, duly deployed, can change delinquents into law-abiding young people. Secondly, it also assumes the legitimacy of a welfare or rehabilitation approach towards delinquency. These two beliefs - that what is required is 'treatment', and that the knowledge about what sort of treatment is required exists - together encourage and, if correct may justify, a transfer of power from the courts to the professionals. While the legitimacy or illegitimacy of the rehabilitative approach is a matter for debate, there can be no doubt that the expertise which can tell us what form of treatment is appropriate for which offender does not exist. What can only be immensely encouraging to those concerned for individual freedom and the life of the spirit, is our failure, as a society, to find any effective ways of changing people.

A third issue which cannot be ignored in discussion of the powers granted to professionals under the 1969 Act is the extent of those powers and the absence of any right of appeal. For example a child might be detained in secure accommodation on grounds of need for many years by the decision of Local Authority social workers without any right of appeal to the court for the child, his parents or guardian (Shepherd, 1977, pp. 80-1). As C.S. Lewis argued many years ago when attacking the humanitarian theory of punishment 'of all tyrannies a tyranny sincerely exercised for the good of its victims may be the most oppressive' (Radzinowicz and Wolfgang, 1971, p. 46).

Another area of professional power and influence closely connected with the powers which social workers exercise under the 1969 Act is the work which social workers and probation officers undertake in the preparation of social inquiry reports for the courts. This work is now a major industry. Reports from probation officers were first used to assist the courts in deciding the suitability of offenders for probation. In 1974 the Home Office encouraged experienced probation officers to make recommendations about sentences in general. 'Now', says Perry (1979, p. 63) the probation officer is 'accepted as an expert adviser over the whole range of sentencing options and their applicability to most of the cases the criminal courts hear.' His advice is 'central to the court's sentencing decision' (ibid., p. 65).

Bean describes the rapid shift in the role of the report writer. 'In 1962', he writes, 'report writers were criticized for expressing "opinions" in their reports; by the late 1960's probation officers were talking openly about making "recommendations" and by the early 1970's they were demanding a "partnership" in sentencing' (ibid., p. 95). Research studies show a varied proportion of the recommendations of social inquiry reports being accepted by the courts but the proportion is clearly large (ibid., p. 6). It is difficult - if not impossible - to know the significance of this. To what extent is the court influenced by the report? To what extent do courts meekly follow recommendations? Or is it that the court shares the same values and views as the social worker? We simply do not know; but it is difficult to believe that over a period of years social inquiry reports are not influential on the general sentencing practices of the courts.

We have seen the powers of social workers under certain provisions of the 1969 Children and Young Persons Act and the potential power accruing to social workers through the expanded industry of social inquiry reports. In the Scottish system of juvenile justice, which is, of course, different from the system in England and Wales, it may well be that the professionals are even more dominant and their power over people even greater.

The key figure in the Scottish system is the Reporter. By background, Reporters tend to be ex-lawyers or ex-social workers. It is the Reporter who decides whether or not a child should be referred to a Hearing by a Children's Panel. The decision is made by the Reporter on the basis of a judgment about whether or not a child is in need of compulsory measures of care. 'Although the Reporter alone is responsible for the decisions to refer the child to the hearing', writes Allison Morris, 'there is no machinery for appeal against it, there are no criteria set out anywhere which might be considered relevant in determining whether or not compulsory measures of care are necessary, the decision is made in private and the Reporter need not give reasons for his decision' (Morris, 1978, p. 97).

The role of social workers in the Scottish system is central. The Reporter's decision as to whether or not to refer the case to a Hearing is made on the basis of a report from the social worker. That same report, or an expanded version, then becomes the focus for discussion at the Hearing. Because of the orientation and ethos of the Hearing it is unlikely to be sharply challenged on any point. Morris's judgment is that while 'English magistrates seem to retain considerable independence in reaching their decisions, panel members, on the other hand, readily accept, possibly because of their training in the values and ethics of social work, the recommendations of social workers' (ibid., p. 117).

The role of psychiatrists in the penal system is another interesting area of professional power over people. In cases of doubt, they have the responsibility of deciding whether or not the accused can reasonably be held responsible for his actions - and therefore whether he can reasonably be punished. The psychiatrist may, of course, recommend medical treatment rather than disposal through the penal system. If commitment is to a mental hospital it may be that years later the psychiatrist has to decide whether or not a violent offender or a murderer should be released. He holds in his hand the man's liberty - and the lives of those in the community potentially at risk if he is released. To leave such decisions to experts imposes on them grave and, at times, almost unbearable responsibilities. The underlying assumption, to which the experts have given support, is that they have the expertise to make such judgments. Whether that is the case is a matter for debate.

Another different kind of power over people which Handler describes in his book 'The Coercive Social Worker' is the increased power accruing to social workers as a result of their power to give material help to families under Section I of the 1963 Children and Young Persons Act. Handler's argument is that when social work help was largely restricted to 'talking' goods, clients felt independent of their social workers and free to reject their advice. When a client, however, received a 'hard' service which he or she needed and valued he felt dependent and less able to reject the social worker's advice in case the help was withdrawn (1973, p. 137). Financial help, Handler found, was often made conditional on a family accepting social work help, such as visits and supervision by a social worker (ibid., p. 67). Given the shortage of Section I monies there had to be rationing. It was only prudence and good husbandry to allocate such resources to those who would make the best use of them - that is to those who would respond to the casework plan (ibid., p. 81). As the Seebohm Report put it in a statement which is relevant both to the kind of professional power we are considering here and to the power implied in the right to define needs and problems 'There is a realisation (produced by growing knowledge and experience) that it is essential to look beyond the immediate symptoms of social distress to the underlying problems' (HMSO, 1968b, para. 141). Only the social worker can bring such insights. The coupling of this kind of assumption with the control over material resources needed by the client gives social workers considerable power over the poorest, weakest and most vulnerable members of society. 'The power to give poor relief', says Jordan, 'becomes quite evidently the most important weapon of authority in the social worker's armoury' (Hill and Laing, 1979, pp. 24-5).

No doubt it is power exercised for people's assumed good, but it is power exercised by some people over other people and it is power against which, if used in an oppressive, arbitrary or inequitable way, there is no redress.

Another interesting and important area of professional power lies in the medical profession's control of the right to abortion under the 1967 Act. That control is absolute and beyond question. Sir George Baker emphasised this in the case of Paton versus the Trustees of the British Pregnancy Advisory Service. There was no case to be considered, Baker concluded 'because it is accepted and common ground that the provisions of the 1967 Act have been complied with. ... My own view is that it would be quite impossible for the courts in any event to supervise the operation of the 1967 Act. The great social responsibility is firmly placed by the law on the shoulders of the medical profession ... not only would it be a bold and brave judge ... who seeks to interfere with the discretion of doctors acting under the 1967 Act, but I think he would really be a foolish judge who would try to do any such thing, unless possibly, there is clear bad faith and an obvious attempt to perpetrate a criminal offence' ((1978) 2 All E.R. 987, pp. 991-2).

Placing the medical profession in this gatekeeping position in relation to abortion has a certain logic. The resource implications of abortion mean that someone has to stand gatekeeper to the health service facilities which are required - though a birth consumes more health resources than an abortion. But in fact, the position which the medical profession occupies in relation to the Act seems to bear little relation to the control of medical resources. Unless there was to be abortion on demand (rather than by need) someone had to make a judgment on the issues involved in determining the right to abortion. The issues seemed close enough to medicine, and the medical profession had a high enough status to make the placing of the responsibility on the doctors look sensible and logical. The result, however, is to give the profession, literally, the power of life or death and to make a moral and political issue into a matter of technical medical judgment.

Psychiatrists, doctors and social workers are not the only groups to have power over people. The professional group which has had the most dramatic effect on the largest number of people in the last thirty years is almost certainly the town planners. We have already made the point that planners, strictly speaking, have influence not power, but their values, concepts, dreams and visions have powerfully affected the lives of many thousands of people.

With their allies and accomplices the environmental health officers and the architects, they have decided on areas for clearance and rehabilitation. Their decisions unfortunately contain a strong element of self-fulfilling prophecy. Planning, in the sense of looking towards the future, means 'lifting' houses. This, in turn, leads to planning blight, which means decay, degeneration and desolation. The planners have it within their power, quite literally, to destroy whole areas of a city - and to effect massive changes in the lives of the people who live there. People may have to move from the house or area where they have spent most of a lifetime. Family ties crucial to physical or emotional well-being may be fractured, community links dissolved, established ways of life transformed out of recognition. Similarly, the planning orthodoxies of the moment, masquerading as a scientific, expert response to a particular situation, powerfully affect people's lives, whether it be high rise, low rise, low density, high density, planned population dispersal or the rehabilitation and revival of the inner city.

The power of the planners to affect people's lives - where they live and how they live, whether they work and where they work, whether they feel a sense of belonging or a sense of alienation - is immense. That power has been fostered and legitimated by the notion which the profession propagated, or at best failed to dispel, that these were issues of expert not political judgment, that really there were no choices. What was proposed by planners, it was assumed, were scientific solutions to the messy problems of human life. Committees and councils bowed before such expertise and assumed all to be for the best.

Teachers too have wide powers over those they teach, power to order their lives in the present and to influence them for the future. Almost inevitably teachers 'label' pupils in their own minds as clever or not so clever, co-operative or uncooperative. Such labelling, and the expectations which are part of it, affect the child's future behaviour as he consciously or unconsciously conforms to those expectations.

The effect of such labelling is most obvious in formal categorisation and streaming systems. These can produce the kind of subcultural attitudes and values which Hargreaves describes so vividly in 'Social Relation in a Secondary School' (1967). The differences he depicts there between A and B streams and C and D streams were substantially the product of school organisation and teacher labelling - and they stand as witnesses to the power of teachers over their pupils. Teachers and schools have a substantial power to mould and influence the values and attitudes of their pupils - accidentally as in the school described by Hargreaves or deliberately in the sense of inculcating particular patterns of attitudes to authority, competition, cooperation, individualism, collectivism, racial and sexual differences. In six or seven hours of daily contact teachers have a major socialising influence. A headteacher and his staff can lay down patterns of dress, haircuts and so on which are acceptable and unacceptable - and heads can suspend those who fail to conform.

The power which the welfare professions exert over people is of varied kinds, but it is clearly considerable. Certainly, there are areas and issues in individual and social life where experts have to decide what action is appropriate and take it. Much professional work is of this kind. Such power can only be justified by expertise. The argument of this section is that such power has expanded into areas where the expertise required to support it does not exist. In that situation professional power over people becomes illegitimate.

V CONTROL OF THE AREA OF WORK

Another type of professional power to which most professional groups aspire is control of the area of work which the profession considers its own. Freidson considers as a crucial element in the definition of a profession the extent to which aspiring occupational groups 'have gained the organised power to control themselves, the terms conditions and content of their work in the settings where they perform their work' (1977, p. 22). Elsewhere, Freidson points out that although professionalism as expertise requires only control of the content of work, professionalism as an expression of prestige presses for control over the organisation of work (1970, p. 143). Few professional groups stop short at the limited objective of control of content of work.

An important element in control of their area of work to which all professions aspire is self regulation of the profession. 'Statutory delegation to professional associations of the power to set and enforce rules of behaviour with the backing of the public law, constitutes the apogee of professional status' says Gilb (1966, p. 136). The recent Committee of Inquiry into the Regulation of the Medical Profession affirmed the entirely professional view, which in fact expressed the current situation, that 'the medical profession should be largely self regulated' because 'we have no doubt that the most effective safeguard of the public is the self respect of the profession itself, and that we should do everything to foster this self respect'(HMSO, 1975, para. 11).

For most of this century the teaching profession has been seeking the establishment of a Teachers' Council analogous to the General Medical Council which would register all qualified teachers and set and enforce standards of entry to the profession. A firm proposal emerged when Edward Short was Secretary of State for Education but it came to grief on the rock of divisions within the profession. Social workers similarly, in the new self confidence of the mid-1970s, began to dream the same dream, seeking the creation of a Social Work Council.

Formal self regulation is a significant element in control over area of work. It is sought for idealistic and ideological reasons - only members of the profession should govern the profession - and for its more tangible but less publicised advantages. It is a step towards control of entry to the profession in terms both of type and number of entrants and it usually embraces control of training. The medical profession has secured victories on all these fronts - violation of the occupational monopoly of the profession in many instances is a crime: the profession itself controls entry to the profession and it controls the content of training. As regards the number of entrants, the profession is in a position in which, though not easily able to stop government reducing the number of entrants, it can prevent expansion of which it disapproves. Teachers and social workers have not yet attained to this level of occupational self control.

Professional control of entry to the medical profession has had certain effects on the composition of the profession. The social class distribution of entrants to medical school can only be regarded as a reflection of the selection policies of those who control entry. The dominance of entrants from Social Classes I and II (Cruikshank and McManus, 1976), is one factor in the subsequent geographical maldistribution of doctors and their shortage in certain areas. Horrobin has argued that other aspects of selection policy are also dysfunctional for the development of medicine. To justify and protect their status, doctors assert implicitly and explicitly the need for high ability to become a doctor. In fact, Horrobin says, 'medicine requires a very modest intelligence' (1978, p. 102), and the recruitment of very able students distorts medical practice by leading to the creation of more and more unnecessary high-powered jobs and to the downgrading of those necessary but ordinary tasks which should make up the greater part of good medical practice.

While any profession should clearly have a strong voice in

decisions about qualifications for entry and for training, it cannot be accepted as a disinterested and objective party to such discussions. All occupational groups have an interest at different times in restricting or expanding entry. Restriction safeguards the prospects of those already aboard the professional ship; expansion is an assertion of the economic and social importance of the profession and may, of course, improve the promotion prospects of existing members. Length of training, too, is a counter to be played by all professions in the game of status and reward seeking - the longer the training the higher the status - so again professional claims need to be treated with a cautious scepticism. Entry qualifications for training or for direct entry to the profession serve the same worthy purpose. Abel Smith, for example, has described how after the Act of Registration in 1919, in spite of changes effected by Parliament, the nursing profession was still able to set educational standards for entry to the profession which were too strict to yield enough nurses to meet all demands 'Such was the toll exacted from society by the professionally-conscious lady nurses' (1975, p. 242). The nurses' concern was with status and the long-term future of the profession. On that altar present patients were sacrificed.

Equally, there are risks in leaving professions to control the content of training. When that happens training can come to reflect a professional idealisation of the work to be done or a particular definition or interpretation of the work rather than the work as it actually is. The aim of all professions is to get their training courses established in universities so they may bathe in what little and fading glory still exists in belonging to those institutions. Universities are implicitly and even explicitly hostile to applied subjects and to training. Professional training in universities suffers from a trend to abstraction, to a stress on education at the expense of training, and to a development on the lines along which non-practising members of the profession would like to see it develop, rather than on the lines dictated by societal needs. Many people would argue that this is what has happened, and is happening, to social work training. Students are being trained for a kind of social work which exists in the minds, memories or imaginations of social work teachers but does not exist in the real world.

In relation to medicine, there is authoritative criticism of the way in which the pattern of training reflects the high prestige sectors of medicine rather than the main emerging health problems of our society. The major health problems today are not medically exciting. The mentally ill, the mentally handicapped, the elderly, the physically handicapped, the chronic sick are poorly represented in our teaching hospitals. But it is here, as McKeown points out, that students acquire their concept of practice. They leave the hospital aspiring to engage in the work they have seen during their training. If 'the largest and most formidable problems by which medicine is now confronted' are isolated from the work of teaching hospitals, a serious gap in medical training is created. McKeown's solution to the problem is that 'the teaching centre should accept responsibility for all medical services for the population of a defined area' (1976, p. 134). Otherwise the interests and concerns of the dominant groups in medicine will continue to bias the nature of training and so the interests and orientation of future entrants to the profession.

Bids for professional monopoly have various implications. They can lead to security of employment for the profession concerned, for its children and its children's children. They can ensure a guaranteed standard of service for consumers who are thus protected from quacks, charlatans and the simply ignorant. On the other hand, there are two potential disadvantages for the community. The first is cost. Studies of the work of different professions - doctors, teachers, social workers, for example - make it quite clear that much of the work done by these professionals does not require their lengthy training, professional skills and substantial salaries. Estimates vary about the proportion of cases dealt with by a GP which could be dealt with quite competently by a trained nurse, but it is considerable. The same is true of the work of social workers. Lengthy training is simply not required for significant parts of the work which social workers undertake. Nevertheless, all professions are reluctant to accept the help of aides and auxiliaries for fear their own position may be compromised. The result of such attitudes is that scarce and expensive professional time is wasted. Professional rates of remuneration are paid for work which does not require professional skills. The taxpayers - and the community - suffer from such a misuse of resources.

The second potential disadvantage for the community lies in the standard of service offered by people who are overtrained and overskilled for what they are tackling. General practitioners produce a continuous and deafening chorus of complaint about the volume of trivial sickness with which they are confronted. Such supposedly trivial complaints might well get much closer and more interested attention from a less trained person. The same point can be made about social work. Staff with less training, selected for their interest and commitment to groups such as the elderly, might well offer them a better service than fully-trained but less interested social workers keen to rush on to the greater attractions of family therapy.

Another element in professional control of the area of work is the ability of a profession successfully to define itself as the key group in the delivery of a particular service. Doctors have persuaded us of two things - one of which is clearly not true and the other of which is dubious. They have persuaded an ever gullible public that they are the crucial element in securing our health - when they are clearly not. Secondly, they have led us to see them as the crucial group in the provision of health services; when we think of health services we think of doctors. In fact, doctors make up only 7 per cent of the NHS's labour force. They are outnumbered by the other health professions. There is the same kind of situation in relation to social workers and social services departments. Social workers make up between 10-15 per cent of the employees of such departments, and yet they have persuaded policy makers and the public that their is the crucial role - a very important achievement.

Another important aspect of the professional's control of his area of work is what happens at the actual meeting of professional and client. At that level too, it seems, the professional is firmly in control. Peggy Foster quotes a study by Byrne and Long which claimed that 'so little of the doctors' behaviour in the consultations which they studied was caused by the patients, that they could analyse almost all of the doctors' verbal behaviour without any reference to the patients as effective agents in the encounters' (1979, pp. 500-1). Strong makes a slightly different point which again illustrates the power relationship between the GP and his patients. 'Their time with the doctor which is their only time', says Strong, 'is not theirs at all. It is at the doctor's disposal and is doled out to them according to unknown criteria' (Davis and Horrobin, 1977, p. 45). An analysis of many social work and probation interviews would almost certainly illustrate the same kind of pattern.

Professionals seek to control entry and training to their profession. They also seek to control the terms and conditions on which they meet with clients and work with them. The meetings are directed rather than exploratory. The professionals retain control at this point just as they seek to control the policy and organisation of the services in which they function.

This lengthy chapter has been concerned with mapping the nature and extent of the power of certain professions in the broad field of social welfare. For the purpose of analysis their power was considered under five headings: power in policy making and administration; power to define needs and problems; power in resource allocation; power over people; and power to control the area of work. There is a widespread reluctance by politicians and administrators to grasp the professional nettle and to assert their authority over and against it. They need the professionals - their work, their expertise, their support. By and large the professionals have done very well in the bargains which have been struck in such relationships. To understand their success, the basis of professional power needs to be examined.

3
The basis of professional power

The concern of this chapter is to examine why it is that the social welfare professions have secured and retained such considerable power and influence over policy making and administration, the definition of needs and problems, resource allocation, people's lives, and their own area of work.

Such power and influence can be explained in terms of the successful self-interested struggles of the occupational groups involved - who sought and secured such authority as they possess for reasons of self-interest - professional, political, psychic and economic. They can also be explained in terms of professional concern for the public interest and the interests of individuals - that such power and influence is necessary as a protection against the omnipresent influence of the omnicompetent state, that it safeguards the professional's right to deliver truly professional services directed to the meeting of professionally defined needs rather than needs defined by state hirelings and bureaucracies.

Five explanations are considered here. First, that the basis of professional power is the alliance of the professions concerned with the state, that is, the union, explicit or implicit, of those groupings formally and informally wielding power in society. Second, that it is the very nature of state welfare services which places the professionals in a position of power. A third set of explanations revolves around the assumed expertise of the professionals. If the issues with which they deal are essentially technical, and if the skills involved are esoteric and beyond the limited comprehension of the laity, then there must be power for professionals, and it is power which must be beyond lay control because beyond lay understanding. The fourth explanation is that power is justified by two elements in the professional's work situation - first by the service ethic, the idea that the professional is essentially motivated by a concern for the welfare of his clients and that he can therefore reasonably be trusted with powers which, if wielded by others, would provoke justifiable anxiety; secondly, it is legitimated by colleague control - the subtle, and at times even explicit, pressures from professional peers to ensure the survival of the highest traditions of professional practice and the due and proper disciplining of that 'rara avis' the professional black sheep. Finally, professional power is based on general public acceptance of the validity and importance of the activity engaged in and the appropriateness of its handling by professionals, and by the unprotesting powerlessness of the groups upon whom, for most of the time, professionals practise their ministrations.

I PROFESSIONS AND THE STATE

The first important point to make about the powers discussed in Chapter 2 is that they are granted explicitly or implicitly by governments. Some professions have to struggle hard to gain the hallmarks of professional status - power to control entry to the profession, legal protection of professional monopoly and peer group control of professional work and standards - and some with professional aspirations fail to secure this acceptance. Crucial, therefore, to an understanding of the basis of professional power is the relationship between the professions and the state.

The relationship varies, of course, from time to time and from place to place. To secure the three crucial powers mentioned above, the profession needs government support and legislation. That much is clear. Not quite so clear, but equally important, is the community of interest which often exists between professions and government. Professions develop because of the importance of the work they do to society or to certain elements within it. Government is therefore going to take an interest in that work, in who does it and how it is done. Pluralist theory would see the professions as powerful groups in the state joining in the competition which has, as its result, the sharing of power and the happy prevention of the dominance of any one interest. Such competition simultaneously welds the professions to the established order and protects the consumer from the worst excesses of unchecked private monopoly.

Functionalist theory, on the other hand, sees the professions as gaining power and privilege because of the functions they perform in society. They operate as the service mechanics of the social system, loosening a bolt here, tightening a screw there. Because they help to keep the ship of state afloat they are given the necessary tools to get on with the job. What the carping and the jealous see as privilege, the functionalist sees quite simply as necessary to the satisfactory performance of a valuable and necessary social task.

Marxist theory takes a quite different view, focusing sharply and clearly on the relationship between professions and the ruling class and seeing professional power as no more than a euphemistic cloak for certain aspects of state power - the power of a class. J.R. Mellor, for example, has argued that the power of town planners is more apparent than real because their ideas have to fit in with ruling interests. Their very image as an autonomous profession is a product of their role in preparing supposedly non-political, technical strategies for furthering ruling interests. Ruling interests want - and need - the world to see planners as important. Sociologists and others have been deluded and 'have taken the profession at its own estimation of authority' ignoring the essential function which its existence serves in capitalist society' (Mellor, 1977, pp. 160-2). As Gramsci argued (1971, p. 260), an alliance between the state and important elements of civil society and the interpretation of the ideas of the one by the other is what gives social democracy its stability. The alliance between the state and the professions, Marxists argue, is just such an alliance.

These three theories all alert us to important dimensions of the relationship between the state and the professions. Pluralist theory helps us to see the professions as powerful interest groups alongside other groups, but it assumes a diversity and distinction between such groups and this needs investigation. Functionalist theory alerts us to the importance of the professions to the smooth running of the social system, but it stops short of the question of whose interests are thus served. Marxist theory suggests a state-profession alliance or rapprochement whereas a more accurate account might emphasise conflict and truce rather than an inevitable identity of interest.

To investigate further the relationship between the professions and the state it is necessary to examine certain aspects of the professions. Clearly the class and status of members of the profession are important. Elliott's argument (1972) is that in Great Britain in law and medicine high status preceded the development of other professional attributes such as expertise and the service ethic. His thesis is that professional autonomy and the powers which go with it flow from the social status of the members of the profession rather than from certain subsequent professional attributes. Marie Haug takes up the point arguing that

> status and autonomy since they were prior conditions, could not have been a consequence of the acquisition of esoteric knowledge. On the contrary, exclusive knowledge and humanitarianist claims can be conceptualised as rationalizations developed to preserve antecedent privileges and power. Thus Elliott's phrase 'status profession,' identifies a critical stage in the development of law, medicine and the clergy, permitting them to carry an indelible stamp of high position into the nineteenth century when they emerged as 'occupational professions' in the context of an industrial society (1975, p. 199).

Professional elites have certainly been well aware of the significance of the class and status of recruits to the profession. Recruits are, of course, potential leaders and to have leaders of the profession who share the same background as leaders in the civil service or in Parliament is of some importance. For other reasons, too, the professions have been concerned about new entrants. As the Royal College of Surgeons put it as recently as 1958 (though the sentiments are those of a more civilised and less egalitarian age)

> there has always been a nucleus in medical schools of students from cultured homes.... This nucleus has been responsible for the continued high social prestige of the profession as a whole and for the maintenance of medicine as a learned profession. Medicine would lose immeasurably if the proportion of such students in the future were to be reduced in favour of the precocious children who qualify for subsidies from the Local Authorities and state purely on examination results (Navarro, 1978, p. 76).

Given the way in which the medical profession controls entry to medical schools such ideas can easily be translated into policy.

The argument is not simply that in class terms the professions are part of the ruling class. That is clearly true for some professions but not for all. There are what might be called the elite professions - for example law and medicine - drawing their members largely from upper- and middle-class groups and historically developing largely in the service of these groups. Then there are the semi, bureaucratic, or sub professions, for example teaching and social work, with members largely recruited from less prestigious social groups and developing within services which do not deal with elite groups in society.

It is possible to argue that while law and medicine secured professional privileges partly because of the status and connections of their members, teachers and social workers, on the other hand, secured rather more limited powers and privileges not because of who they were, but because of the value of their work to the maintenance of a particular economic and social system. They were useful - as too were law and medicine - in the furtherance of the central purposes of the capitalist state, the reproduction of labour, the preservation of property and the control of deviance (Johnson, 1977).

The way in which key professions have defined the problems with which they deal is also important in the context of the connection between professions and government. The professions have contributed to a depoliticising of social problems, treating them rather as personal problems susceptible to individual solution by experts. The growth of a host of helping professions has implicitly propagated the notion that the problems with which they deal could be solved within the existing pattern of economic and social relations, that such problems were marginal, technical and susceptible to solution by appropriate prescriptions of modern medicine, or the latest planning, educational or social work orthodoxies. Such scientific judgments immediately announced the professionals as men of judgment and perception and as reliable allies in the task of maintaining the existing social order. 'By locating the source and the treatment of problems in an individual', says Zola writing of medicine as an institution of social control, 'other levels of intervention are effectively closed' (Cox and Mead, 1975, p. 182). Such an approach naturally commends the profession to those with an interest in maintaining the existing economic and social order. Powers and privileges were the due and proper reward for endeavours to solve insoluble problems in a society which perpetuated them.

The professions have always had their friends and spokespersons in crucial rooms in the corridors of power.

Bottoms, as we have seen, explains the passing into law of the Children and Young Persons Act 1969 - an important step in the growth and acceptance of social work as an emerging profession - as the product of a conjunction of interests and ideology between the British Labour Party and those in key positions in British social work. Crucial too was the emergence of a group of civil servants in the upper reaches of the Children's Department of the Home Office who were committed to a 'child care' or 'professional' view of delinquency (Bottoms, 1974, p. 322 ff.). They had learned this view from social science and social work research and writing. Because they were attuned to the social work ideas of the moment, they pushed hard for a measure which gave social workers a more significant role in the field of delinquency. For our present purposes the crucial point is the alliance between a profession and groups of politicians and civil servants with a key role in the policy making process. This same alliance was also a crucial factor in the implementation of the Seebohm Report.

Klein pinpoints the essential nature of the relationship between the medical profession and government. 'To think of the medical and health professions as pressure groups working from outside the system', he writes, 'is to miss much of the point. The relationship between the central bureaucracy and the health professions is symbiotic.... Thus, in the context of the NHS it would probably be fairer to talk about the professionalisation of the bureaucracy than the bureaucratisation of the medical service' (Navarro, 1978, p. 127). Klein does not make plain how he explains this symbiotic relationship. Navarro is quite explicit that in his view the crucial factor is the common class origins and class positions of those in the central bureaucracy and in the key positions in the health professions (ibid.). Common interests and mutual need may be a sounder explanation. Class is one element in such a situation but it is too much of a shorthand explanation to bring out the full variety and strength of the links.

The relationship however is plain and is neatly illustrated by the position of the Chief Medical Officer in the Department of Health and Social Security. He has independent right of access to the Minister. He publishes his own annual report 'On The State of the Public Health'. On the basis of recent years he is likely to be in post longer than either the Minister or the Permanent Secretary - which inevitably increases his influence. He acts as Medical Officer to the Home Office and the Department of Education and Science and advises the Ministry of Agriculture and the Department of the Environment on medical matters. 'Such pre-eminence, being given to one member of a particular profession', says Ruth Levitt, 'is unique within the Civil Service, and is a significant acknowledgment of the medical profession's power and influence' (1976, p. 37).

Another interesting example of the importance of political connections is the way in which certain policies dear to the hearts of the teaching profession were pushed forward while Edward Short, a card-carrying member of the NUT, was Secretary of State for Education and Science. There were two significant victories - first when the Union persuaded the Secretary of State to end the employment of unqualified teachers in schools. Kogan calls it the Union's 'most significant victory' (1975, p. 108). The other victory, though in the end it yielded no fruit, was in relation to the historic struggle for a Teachers' Registration Council to govern the teaching profession. Sixty years of intermittent agitation had produced nothing till Short arrived at the DES and promptly set up a working party to look at the idea. It reported in favour of such a Council and proposed a body dominated by nominees of the major teachers' associations. In the end, however, the proposal broke apart after rejection by the NUT and the ATTI and a change of government (Coates, 1972, p. 53). For a time the teachers seemed close to attaining one of the ultimate accolades of professional acceptability - effective self government - and what brought this within their grasp was their political connections.

The links between the professions and the state are those of interest, class, ideology and mutual dependence. Occupations develop because what they do is useful to someone, or meets a need - genuine or manufactured. Professions evolve for just such reasons, but all depend for their development on state action whether that action be the organisation of services, the provision of finance or the creation of professional monopolies. Equally the state needs professions to fulfil the responsibilities which modern governments assume, to legitimate state power, to make available expertise, to deal with the common situations of industrial society. The state and the professions need each other, their functions and powers have grown side by side in an alliance at different times firm and precarious, explicit and implicit. That mutual need is at the basis of the power of the professions in social welfare. Although a near monopoly employer of the key welfare professions, democratic governments are not in a position easily to coerce them. Given the standing of the professions, and their expertise, any such action would look too much like tyranny so the norm is a relationship of mutual accommodation.

II THE PROFESSIONS AND STATE WELFARE

It can be argued that the involvement of government with welfare programmes contributes substantially to the power of the welfare professions. State involvement underpins the growth of planning, medical services, education and personal social services. It leads, therefore, to an expansion of the relevant professions and to an increase in their importance and in their self confidence. 'When we survey the successive stages in the growth of membership and power of particular professional organisations', the Webbs wrote in 1917, 'we see these stages nearly always marked by some concurrent increase of state activity in the same service' (Klein, 1973b, p. 4).

The important role of the professions in the delivery of key services means that government comes to depend on the professions for the implementation of its commitments. As the BMA pointed out to Bevan in 1946 'You need the doctors, we have the doctors.' Also, given public interest and concern for the services, the professions can appeal to popular support over the heads of government - what Manzer describes as 'electoral' power as distinct from the 'technical' power resulting from expertise (1970, p. 56). State welfare policies also inevitably involve government in concern about the quality of the services delivered. This gives a new force to the demand which all professions make at some stage in their development for the practice of particular activities to be restricted to those with specific professional qualifications - the claim for monopoly. The profession argues that this is the only way for government to guarantee the quality of the services provided. If the profession can gain a monopoly of a particular service, then that is an important step towards the goal of full professional status. It is also an important source of power. 'Knowledge itself does not give special power', says Friedson, 'only exclusive knowledge gives power to its possessors' (Haug, 1975, p. 198).

Public involvement in welfare provides, therefore, certain possibilities for the professions. It also emphasises the mutual need which links professions and government. The privileges - rights as the professions see things - which the professions claim can only be granted and enforced by government. Only government, too, can guarantee continuing employment for many of the new professionals; they are the offspring and the beneficiaries of welfare state policies. On the other hand, government needs the professions - both, as we have seen, to implement the policies to which it is pledged, and also to advise it on how particular aims might be achieved and how services might best be organised. Only the professions have the knowledge and experience which government needs to create and sustain the complex edifice of social welfare provision. The result is that members of the key welfare professions assume significant positions in the hierarchies of the relevant departments of state and the professional associations become almost a part of government - assuming the symbiotic relationship which Klein describes as the only way to understand the profession - government connection. That particular relationship is the direct result of welfare state policies.

Another important way in which state social services increase professional power is that with public acceptance of financial responsibility for the services, and so for the professions concerned, the professions no longer depend on clients for their income. They no longer have to please their clients to maintain their financial security. They have secured a crucial measure of independence from public judgment. Certainly, the state still has to be satisfied about competence and integrity, but in a free public system the more immediate power of the client is greatly diminished - for good and ill. The professional is freed to concentrate solely on the client's needs, but on the other hand he is freed from the immediate necessity of providing a service which responds to his client's wishes.

Another feature of state welfare which serves to underpin the power and authority of the professions engaged in delivering such services is its bureaucratic nature. Much has been written about the conflicts which face professionals who work in bureaucracies. Less has been written on how bureaucracies can free professionals from many of the constraints and inhibitions of single-handed private practice and support and increase professional authority. 'To the extent that the professional becomes part of an administrative machine', says Klein, '- whether this be the NHS, the town planning department of a local authority or the legal staff of a government ministry - so his command over resources, and his ability to affect the consumer, is magnified' (Klein, 1973b, p. 5). It is, for example, only a publicly financed health service which can make clinical freedom a reality for the doctor.

In the field of social welfare, supply creates demand. While resources are always limited, the human ability to gobble up health, education and personal social services is virtually limitless. The result is the need to ration services, to balance supply and demand according to some criteria of need. At a time of expenditure cuts and standstills the key role of the professionals in rationing services becomes crucial to the quality of life of more and more people. Such decisions have to be made by experts in a society which seeks to make such judgments on the basis of need. Often, indeed, the professionals are left to draw up the rules about priorities, which is a political rather than a professional task, as well as making decisions about individual cases on the basis of agreed general principles.

Another characteristic of professional work in social welfare which increases the power of professionals is that much work is inherently difficult to supervise. If the service is designed to meet needs rather than expressed desires there can be no prior inspection of the service by the client or indeed by anyone else; he has to accept the professional's services in good faith or reject them in advance. Professionals generally provide an individualised service which increases the difficulty of supervision. 'Doctors have clinical autonomy in the NHS', Tolliday argues, 'because although state provided, the policy for NHS care is that of personalized care.' It is this policy of providing personal care 'that gives doctors their right to unmanaged status' (Tolliday, 1978, p. 37). Again, professionals deal with clients in private, or in situations where external observation is difficult. The confidentiality of the relation, while supposedly designed to protect the client, also protects the professional. Routine standardised procedures are impossible where an individual service is being delivered. Such a situation means that professionals must have freedom and discretion over the course of action they pursue. At the same time this increases their independence and their power.

In general, in the social welfare field it is difficult to set objectives or to evaluate the output of services. This weakens the power of bureaucrats and administrators and increases the power of the front-line professionals. Frequently, too, the administrators are conscious of this and accept the need of the professional providers for freedom to make their own judgments about priorities. Many professionals too - for example general practitioners or social workers or teachers - work in decentralised settings which makes control of their day-to-day activities impossible. Providers can also assert the undeniable fact that they are in closer touch than anyone else with the needs the service seeks to meet and that they therefore need freedom to deal flexibly with the situations they confront.

Also important in the evolution of professional power is the dominance of certain attitudes and ideologies in state welfare provision. They are in part the result of the influence of the professionals and in part the cause of the rise of the professionals. The definition of problems as personal rather than structural is an assertion of the importance of the role of professionals in their treatment. The definition of problems of health, delinquency and mental illness as personal is both a product of the power of the professions to shape societal ideologies and attitudes and a fillip to the role of professionals in their treatment.

The belief that treatment by experts is the appropriate response to a range of situations and problems gives the professional a crucial role. If treatment is to fit the criminal not the crime, then expert, professional judgments have to be made. This exalts the power and status of those with such skills. 'The functioning of the therapeutic state', says Kittrie, 'is dependent upon an atmosphere which de-emphasises the overt act and permits the needs of the offender to dictate the length of his confinement and the measure of his treatment' (1971, p. 374). Such an approach gives the experts great power. A system which deals with deviance simply by punishment has no need of experts - except in the rather narrowly specialised field of the technology and techniques of punishment. Punishment is according to dessert and that is a matter of judgment requiring little technical expertise. The belief that what is required is treatment and that there are people with the skills and techniques to administer such treatment, does much for the power and status of the groups making such claims.

The final element in welfare ideology which serves to strengthen professional power is the assertion and encouragement of the notion that certain important parts of life are properly delegated to professionals, as their responsibility. Health is a matter for doctors, the care of certain special needs groups is properly the responsibility of social workers, education is the responsibility of teachers. Inevitably, definition of a problem in terms of a need for professional intervention extends the sphere of professional power and influence. We become, in Illich's terms, the medicalised, schooled, profession-dependent society having lost the power to cope on our own with basic human needs and situations. Such delegation leads to disablement. The professionals edge towards control of a larger area of our lives.

Education is an interesting example of this notion. The Plowden Committee was struck by how much more closely parents in other countries were usually associated with schools, both formally and informally (HMSO, 1967, para. 123). The tradition of non-involvement of parents in the United Kingdom is strong and can be attributed to the powerful and pernicious influence of the public schools. In such establishments the teachers had to operate 'in loco parentis' rather than 'cum parente'. By a process of emulation and osmosis this became the pattern in the rest of the school system bringing with it both the blessing of the tradition of pastoral care in British schools and the hostility and ambivalence towards parental involvement. As Young and McGeeney point out 'The British ideal is of the surrogate parent, and if one is setting oneself up as that, the presence of the real parent may be nothing but an embarrassment' (1968, p. 112). So a particular tradition and ideology in education buttresses the power of the professionals.

The argument of this section has been that the nature of state-provided welfare services, for a range of reasons, contributes to the power of professionals in our society. Professional power has marched hand in hand with public welfare. Professionals gain the power which arises from being needed by government if political commitments are to be fulfilled. They gain the power which flows from work which is inherently difficult to supervise. They climb up on the crest of certain ideologies which feed the growth of welfare and are nourished by it. They bathe in the reflected power of the organisations in and from which they work, and by virtue of the crucial decisions which they have to make about access to, and eligibility for, services. The strands in the fabric of welfare which, when knitted together, form a basis for professional power are diverse. The basis they form is, however, extremely solid.

III THE PROFESSIONS AND THEIR EXPERTISE

Clearly the expertise to which the professionals lay claim is important in the origin and justification of the power which they wield. The precise connection between expertise and power needs, however, to be explored. I shall argue that expertise contributes to professional power in six different ways.

First of all expertise is associated with power in our society because of our faith in what Parsons calls 'the primacy of cognitive rationality' (1949, ch. 2). We believe in the value and importance of expertise, and those who claim it and display it gain status, influence and power. 'Professionals profess.', says Everett Hughes, 'They profess to know better than others the nature of certain matters, and to know better than their clients what ails them and their affairs. This is the essence of the professional idea and the professional claim' (Gartner and Riessman, 1974, p. 157). This is equally true of the accepted and the aspirant professions - the claim to expertise serves in our society to justify power and authority. Simmie, for example, emphasises the way in which town planners have relied on the claim to expertise and rationality to support their policy prescriptions. He writes of the 'widespread contemporary belief among planners that planning is virtually synonymous with rationality' (1974, p. 161). Rationality and expertise are very difficult to challenge in a society which depends so heavily upon them; they therefore bring power and influence.

It is faith in knowledge which underpins the powers given to the medical profession to deal with the mentally ill, or the power given to social workers and probation officers to deal with delinquents. There is faith that knowledge exists or can be developed and that it can be applied to solve problems.

The second point to be made about professional expertise and the way it functions to support claims to power is that the expertise claimed by the social welfare professions is of individual and social importance. It is a particular kind and quality of expertise. 'Professional men collectively', Carr-Saunders wrote fifty years ago, 'possess the ability to perform all those skilled services upon which the continued functioning of modern society depends' (Vollmer and Mills, 1966, p. 4). It is knowledge about life and death, mental, physical and social well-being, the healing of individual and social ills, the preservation of the economic and social order to which the professions lay claim.

Such expertise necessarily makes for a close functional relationship between the professions and government. This is clearly true of the medical profession and health. It is also true of teachers. 'Technical power' (the power teachers exercise by virtue of their knowledge and the need government has for their cooperation), says Manzer, 'is a continuing factor in securing a voice for the teaching profession in making educational policy' (1970, p. 56). Governments need and value such knowledge. Those who possess it, possess a currency of political value.

Thirdly, the possession of such expertise is used to justify various classic professional claims: for monopoly, because only members of the profession have the expertise required to tackle that particular work; to control of entry to the profession, because only those who have professional expertise can judge the fitness of candidates for admission to the professional ranks; to pronounce authoritatively on major areas of public policy, because only they have the requisite knowledge to make informed judgments. Such claims and the powers which they yield can have important effects on the development of whole areas of social policy. Once the professional claim to control entry to the profession and to determine the pattern of training is accepted, then professional definitions of needs and problems are also by implication accepted. A series of seemingly logical steps, in view of the expertise which is claimed, lead to a position in which political powers are effectively abdicated.

An example of the effect of this power is the system of Distinction Awards to consultants in the National Health Service. Awards are made on the advice of the Advisory Committee on Distinction Awards, a predominantly professional body. The justification for the professional dominance of the Committee is the obvious one that only doctors know what constitutes good doctoring. On the other hand, the system does much more than hand out extra money to men of great distinction. In Klein's words, 'it tends to perpetuate, and reinforce, an order of prestige within the medical profession' (1973a, p. 325). In 1977, in England and Wales, 73 per cent of consultants in thoracic surgery, 64 per cent of those in cardiology and 67 per cent of those in neurosurgery held awards compared with only 23 per cent of those in geriatrics, 25 per cent of those in mental health and 26 per cent in rheumatology and rehabilitation (HMSO, 1979, para. 14.96). The profession is, in effect, being allowed to decide which branches of medicine shall be picked out for extra reward and prestige. The selection it makes helps to influence the pattern of development of medicine, of medical priorities and resource use.

The fourth way in which expertise contributes to professional power is indirectly, through the subtle effects of the lengthy formal training required to acquire such expertise. The training is explicitly to inculcate knowledge and implicitly to establish a professional identity. The training experience produces a professional solidarity and the self confidence which professionals need to perform their work. It brings, too, a faith in the correctness of the narrow corpus of professional knowledge and this gives professionals a confidence and authority which undergirds the power they exercise. This argument can be related usefully to social work. The claim for a scientific knowledge base, Jones suggests, helps to sustain the social worker in the belief he is doing right, just as it communicates to the client who fails to follow his social worker's advice that what he is doing is wrong. Scientific knowledge and a theory of human behaviour (whether correct or not) is a far more effective prop to authority than a reliance on simple moral categories (Parry, Rustin and Satyamurti, 1979, p. 80).

Haug reports that her research on general practitioners in the UK showed many examples of doctors tending to define questioning of their expertise as neurotic - which is a fruit of the overweening confidence produced by professional training and socialisation (1975, pp. 203-4). Fennell describes a similar kind of professional interpretation of reality which he saw during his research on Mental Health Review Tribunals. If a patient disputed any facts stated by the psychiatrist, this was interpreted as part of his symptomatology unless he could find someone to substantiate his story. If he attempted to deny that he was getting treatment, that was to show a lack of insight. 'The psychiatrist', Fennell writes, 'possesses the ultimate weapon of the ability to explain away attacks on his opinion of the patient, by relegating these attacks to the status of symptomatology' (1977, p. 218). Social workers, too, are all too ready to describe clients who disagree with their interpretation of their situation as lacking in insight. Though 'the client may mean what he says, he doesn't know what he means' (Pearson, 1975, p. 130). Such ability to reinterpret criticism by the patient is, of course, the ultimate weapon against any attack on professional expertise. It degrades the understanding and rationality of the client and ascribes to the professional's expertise an unchallengeable status. To describe someone's views as neurotic or lacking in insight is to dismiss them as altogether beneath consideration. Professional training and socialisation help create this view of the world which underpins such attitudes and contributes so notably to professional authority and self confidence.

While the professions assert the expertise of individuals, they also lay great stress on the collective expertise of the profession as such. This assertion supports the power and authority of individual members. The individual professional knows himself to be heir to a rich inheritance. He also, as an individual, benefits from the assumed collective expertise of the profession to which he belongs. If experts have admitted people for professional training and the training has been conducted by experts, then the output must be expert. The logical assumption is then that all professionals, once licensed, are competent. Through licensing 'competence becomes an attribute of the profession as a whole, rather than of individuals as such' (Hughes, 1958, pp. 141-2).

Freidson makes a further, analogous point about the nature of professional competence. What is sought, he suggests

> even demanded - by the profession is that the client obeys because he has faith in the competence of his consultant without evaluating the grounds of the consultant's advice. ... Stress is on the necessity of faith or trust in the practitioner - in short, on <u>imputed</u> rather than demonstrated competence. A professional's advice should be obeyed because it is a professional who gives it, not because the advice can be evaluated on its evidential merits. Here we find the special source of the authority of the profession - incumbency in an expert status (Wrong, 1979, p. 54).

The last way in which expertise is related to professional power is that the claim for expertise is accompanied by the assertion and assumption that the professional is always competent and correct unless and until proved otherwise. This frees the professional from routine review of his performance.

A profession's belief in its own expertise makes it sceptical of all evaluation, and contemptuous and dismissive of any attempt at evaluation by those who are not members of the profession, and who have not imbibed its sacred mysteries.

This general scepticism about evaluation is rooted in the belief that individually and collectively professionals know what is effective and what is not. In a sense, what is being asserted is that professional work is beyond evaluation by any normal processes of assessment apart from the judgment of the particular professional involved, because no one else can know the situation as he does - and by virtue of his membership of the profession he is competent to judge it.

Expertise, then, is a barrier to critical evaluation both because of the normal difficulties of evaluating the work of individual experts and because of the odour of sanctity which is cultivated by the professions and surrounds them and is produced partly by the nature of their assumed expertise. Even professional evaluation, however, is unpopular. No one, of course, positively enjoys evaluation. To be able to avoid it, or keep it to a minimum, is an indication of power and prestige - and expertise is at the root of this ability. The medical profession has been able to restrict evaluation of its work because of faith in the expertise of its members - that what is done by individual doctors in individual cases is the best that could be done. Review is therefore unnecessary, and by a process of moral extrapolation, illegitimate.

The professions' claim to expertise is a vital element in the power they wield. It gives them authority in their various spheres of activity. It makes them important to government, for their expertise is regarded as useful in furthering the purposes of the modern state. It gives them a standing and a status in the eyes of those who use their services, so legitimating their authority and privileges and enabling them to dismiss complaints as the product of ignorance and misunderstanding. It makes substantial autonomy in their area of work entirely logical because no one but another professional has the knowledge to control and organise their work. Expertise can also be stretched unobtrusively from technical expertise to expertise in the organisation of that expertise, so feeding professional imperialism. On its own, expertise does not bring power - it has to be useful expertise which is valued by government, and it has to provide guarantees that it will be used only for achieving acceptable purposes in acceptable ways - but without it no aspirant profession can make progress.

IV MORAL VERACITY, THE SERVICE ETHIC AND COLLEAGUE CONTROL

No government could or would grant the professions the powers and freedoms they enjoy without some guarantees about their use. The professions offer three such guarantees all of which are used in the struggle to obtain recognition as an established profession. Government subsequently uses the same arguments to justify the powers granted to professions. They can, therefore, reasonably be regarded as making up part of the basis of professional power.

Firstly, there is the generally accepted claim to what Pearson calls 'moral veracity' (1975, p. 69); secondly, there is the service ideal, what Wilensky calls 'the pivot around which the moral claim to professional status revolves' (1964, p. 140); and thirdly, there is colleague control of the individual professional.

These systems of control form part of the basis of professional power because they purport to provide guarantees of how such power will be used. They encourage and justify the granting of independence and power to professionals because of the assurance they provide that power over people or resources will not be misused, but will be employed only in the service of clients and the common good, not for selfish professional advantage or aggrandisement.

The great powers which professionals have over people could only be granted by government and gain general acceptance if the professions possessed public trust, corporately and individually. Belief in the professions' disinterested concern is basic to trust, and trust is quite crucial to the client-professional relationship. In economic relationships caveat emptor is a principle which retains a hint of realism. In professional relationships, given the expertise on one side and the client's ignorance on the other, given the stress that the professional deals with needs rather than desires, given the impossibility of predicting the outcome of certain kinds of intervention, a marked scepticism has to give way to trust. Without trust, the personal service and social welfare professions - law, medicine, social work, teaching and planning could not have developed. They have all laid claim to 'moral veracity' and to trust and, as McKinlay points out, 'This claim to trust is almost universally accepted in Western societies' (1973, p. 66). It is concern to preserve the reputation for trustworthiness which undergirds the great anxiety in all professions over professional misconduct, the abuse of trust in the client-professional relationship. That is the ultimate professional sin, regarded much more seriously than incompetence, because, without trust, the power - and privileges - of the professionals would become unacceptable and many cherished freedoms would have to be reined in. The assumption underlying the freedom which professionals enjoy, for example, under the 1959 Mental Health Act, is that the professionals can be relied upon to act only in the best interests of the patient.

The second control on the way professionals operate is the service ethic to which all professions and would-be professions lay vigorous claim. The essence of the professional claim here is that the main aim of the professions is not personal or collective profit and advantage, but service to their clients and to the community. The extent to which ethical codes and the ideal of service are real influences on professional behaviour is not important at this point. Our concern is with the significance of the stated ideal of service in the implicit contract between the professional and society, and its importance in legitimising certain professional powers and privileges. Some commentators argue that codes of ethics are political counters constructed as much to serve as public evidence of professional intentions and ideals as to provide actual behavioural guidelines for practitioners (McKinlay, 1975, p. 308). Others, Wilensky for example, insist that 'the norm of selflessness is more than lip service. It is probably acted out in the established professions at a somewhat higher rate than in other occupations' (1964, p. 140). The important point is that the service ethic is a powerful justification of power and privilege. In Freidson's words, it is a 'pre-requisite for being trusted to control the terms of work without taking advantage of such control' (1970b, p. 360). The profession therefore cannot afford to see the code breached too clearly or too often. It is the 'quid' which the profession offers for the 'quo' of government-granted freedom, and a reasonable measure of conformity to it is the price to be paid for wider freedom.

Colleague control is a kind of intermediate method of professional accountability coming between the individual responsibility produced by moral veracity and the service ideal, and the full panoply of a system of bureaucratic control through rules, checks and balances. The principle of colleague control is the justification for professional freedom from other kinds of control. The profession is granted a very substantial measure of self government and self control, both because its claim that it can be trusted is largely accepted, and because supervision in other ways would be extremely difficult. The idea of formal colleague- or peer-group control at various levels from national - the General Medical Council, to local - local medical committees, and informal control through the socialisation process or the immediate work group, is a kind of corporate guarantee of professional trustworthiness and a longstop answer to the problem of the individual deviant professional.

The reality of colleague control at the formal or informal level may be questionable but it is vigorously asserted by the British Medical Association, for example, when there is talk of other forms of control. 'The whole professional life and pattern of work of the doctor and dentist in the NHS hospital service', the BMA argued recently, 'is such as to maintain high standards and to expose him constantly in his work and results to the scrutiny of colleagues, from whom the truth cannot be concealed - even if he at any time desired so to do' (HMSO, 1977a, p. 61). What matters here is the significance of the principle as a factor legitimating professional power. It legitimates government inaction when effective supervision would be extremely difficult, and it enables government to argue that it has not neglected its responsibility to the consumer of professional services because their interests are, in fact, safeguarded. The powers of the professions have to seem reasonable. The nature of state welfare services and the extent of professional expertise are a pragmatic form of justification - 'that's how in the real world it has to be'. Moral veracity, the service ethic and colleague control provide a justification in principle.

V PROFESSIONAL POWER AND PUBLIC ACCEPTANCE

'Over the past fifty years', writes Yablonsky, 'the treatment of social problems has been dropped into the professional lap and has been held onto tightly. The propaganda about the professional's exclusive right to treat social problems has reached its high mark. The professionals, the public, and even patients are firmly convinced that the only "bona fide" treatments and "cures" available come from "legitimate professionals" with the right set of degrees' (Horowitz and Liebowitz, 1968, p. 283). Two questions are suggested by this statement and they form the focus of this section. First, how great is public support for the professions? Second, what is the explanation for this acceptance of the professional claim? It is an important issue because its acceptance by governments, and more generally in society, is part of the basis of the power the professions wield. As we shall see in the next chapter, that acceptance is less general and less firm today than it has been in the past, but it is still an important factor underpinning the power of the professions.

Glennerster writes of 'the general consensus, perhaps more strongly held in the British public services than the American, that the professions, in their day to day dealings with clients, pupils or patients, ought to be the final arbiter of the values, purposes and priorities inherent in their activity' (1975, p. 31). It is easy to produce examples of such a consensus. One of the three Chief Education Officers interviewed in 'County Hall', for example, said quite explicitly that he did not think it was his responsibility to insist on developments in the schools which the teachers themselves were not prepared to accept (Kogan and van der Eyken, 1973, p. 54). The powers given to doctors and social workers which were discussed in Chapter 2 illustrate the same attitude. Such public confidence is crucial to the power of professionals in policy making, and to the freedom and discretion they exercise in their day-to-day work.

Abel Smith comments on the importance of the high popular standing of the medical profession as a factor in the decisions surrounding the creation of the National Health Service. 'When the community took over responsibility for its hospitals in 1948', he says, 'the entrenched power and privilege of professional interests became matters in which government had a direct interest. But Ministers did not dare to challenge a profession which had by now too high a standing in the eyes of public opinion' (1975, p. 248). The same point was made by the editors of the 'Yale Law Journal' in their classic examination of the political basis of the power of the American Medical Association. Their conclusion was that 'the political strength of the AMA is to a large degree attributable to the status of the doctor in society' and that public trust 'unchallenged in the realm of medical science, extends also into the economic and political aspects of health' ('Yale Law Journal', 1954, p. 94).

A specific example of public acceptance of the power and influence of the medical profession is the actual shape and nature of the National Health Service Act 1946. Eckstein describes it as 'skeletal'. It provided a framework and left the Minister, the civil servants, and the medical profession to put the flesh on the bare legislative bones. Such an approach by Parliament, Eckstein argues, 'denotes its willingness to abdicate its own influence (and the influence of party) to that of technically specialised groups' (1960, p. 156). Such an abdication expresses acceptance of the trustworthiness and power of the professional groups involved and must reflect a broader societal acceptance.

The subsequent history of the NHS shows other examples of this acceptance of professional power and independence. The history of health centre policy, Phoebe Hall concludes 'illustrates the reluctance of civil servants to interfere in any positive way with the autonomy of the medical profession. Once antipathy towards health centres was demonstrated by general practitioners, government officials were content to await a change of mind rather than attempt to enforce it' (1975, p. 309). The same attitude is exemplified in the comment of the American New Deal social welfare planner Edwin E. Witte, made in the light of AMA opposition to health insurance - 'As long as the medical profession is opposed, we will not have health insurance ... I am willing to let the profession decide' (Heidenheimer, 1973, p. 333). Public acceptance of professional power needs to be explored at a number of levels - at the level of government and at the level of public opinion and popular attitudes, at the level of policy making, administration and accountability, and at the level of interaction with individual clients and users. Certain general reasons can, however, be suggested for the widespread acceptance of the professional claim for power and influence.

Government acceptance of the role of the professions in policy making, resource allocation and administration is partly the result of dependence on the professionals to run services, partly the result of government's need for expertise, and partly the result of the general, if ill-defined, belief that the professionals should have a major say in their conditions of work and the organisation of services. In other words, government accepts the professional claim, partly from necessity, partly because of ideology. Government and the professions have shared interests and needs, a kind of bargain is struck - power and influence in return for expertise and support in the running of services. In turn, broader public acceptance of the professional claim owes something to the close relationship between government and the professions. Because government grants the professions power and influence, popular opinion accepts the professional position.

Another important factor in governmental and public acceptance of the power and influence of the professions is belief in the importance of their work. If doctors really do have power over life and death, if the Merrison Committee is right in its naive assertion that 'The health of the nation will be founded on the cornerstone of the wise and responsible practice of medicine' (HMSO, 1975, para. 24), and if the power, resources and freedoms we give the medical profession are used to further life, then we should give them all they ask for. It seems this is how people feel. 'Most lay people', says Horrobin, 'feel that apart from doctors' salaries what the profession wants is likely to be in the public interest.' He goes on to pinpoint the significance of this when he says, 'I agree absolutely that this is one of the mainsprings of the power of medicine' (Horrobin, 1978, p. 43).

Faith in the expert knowledge of the profession is crucial to its public acceptance. The expert knowledge needs, too, to contain an element of mystery, of visibility and yet invisibility, and to be related to situations which are of vital importance to people's lives. Teachers will never gain the same level of acceptance for their claims to professional power as doctors because we have all observed them in action for fifteen thousand hours, and it is difficult for mystery to survive such a prolonged and debilitating exposure. Equally, social workers claim to deal with life and death situations, but, whereas with doctors - as a rather crude generalisation - we only hear of their successes, with social workers, the opposite is true; we only hear of their failures - Maria Colwell and the other tragedy victims. If social workers have specialised knowledge, it does not mesh effectively with the types of knowledge which have high status in a scientific, technological society. Also, social workers generally only deal with those with low status in society. Their work may be useful to the rest of us, in taming the deviant and minimising the tragedies which disturb our moral digestions, but it is not of the same manifest general value as the work of doctors. On the other hand, in such a situation the powers which tender-minded civil servants and politicians grant to social workers are not going greatly to trouble the general public.

It is interesting that although teachers lack the standing

and status of doctors, there is no sign of any significant movement of parents or politicians to challenge their position in the education system. There may be popular concern about the content of courses and modern methods of teaching, but there is sufficient acceptance of the professional authority of teachers to inhibit any significant action to reduce teacher autonomy.

Another factor in public acceptance of professional power is the professional claim - explicit or implicit - that what is claimed is claimed purely on the basis of knowledge and for the sake of service. Where that claim can be established, then interference by non-professionals is clearly both an intrusion and potentially damaging to the professional's clients. The only course for rational men is to accept the profession's demands. The influence of town planners was so great in the 1950s and 1960s because they swathed their proposals in the wraps of rationality and expertise - which in a rational society makes them beyond challenge. Doctors legitimise all their claims by the assertion that what is at issue is good medical practice and in general the professions' assertion that they exist to serve seems accepted. Trustworthiness must be established if powers and privileges are to be accepted.

Acceptance of professional power in the immediate professional-client relationship owes something to all these factors. It also owes something to class deference. Most users of professional services are of less education and lower social class than the professionals with whom they deal. They meet them in situations where the terms of the encounter, be it GP's consulting room, hospital, social work interview, school, or meeting to discuss planning proposals, are dictated by the professionals rather than the clients. They meet, too, over issues where the professionals are knowledgeable and in situations which the professionals are experienced in managing, and where the client is ignorant, helpless or needy. The client is in the position of supplicant. He seeks advice and help and often he can only gain access to the goods and services he needs to improve his situation from the professional. He has been told many times how busy the professional is. To ask questions and seek information beyond what the professional offers, requires courage, persistence and a measure of selfishness.

In such situations users of the social services are, in Pinker's words, 'paupers at heart' (1971, p. 142). They have little sense of a right to be heard, or of a right to a particular quality of service. They lack the equality of class, status or knowledge, or the group organisation, which might enable them to confront the professional on a more equal footing. The client has been schooled to a belief in experts - one of the more dangerous of contemporary ideologies. Disabled by such schooling, he seeks someone who will tell him what he needs and how to achieve it. The 'client', Greenwood suggests, 'derives a sense of security from the professional's assumption of authority' (Vollmer and Mills, 1966, p. 13). Powles speaks of the technology of modern medicine as meeting, in addition to people's biological needs, 'the emotional and existential challenges that disease involves' (1973, p. 20) in a secular society. The client becomes dependent on the profession at a range of levels. The professions emphasise all they can do, the client sees the wisdom of putting his health, his children or the future of his neighbourhood, into the expert and trustworthy hands of the professional. He is schooled to consume services, to passivity, rather than to participate in dialogue about the situation which is the subject of concern.

Another factor underpinning this kind of dependent relationship, which in turn makes for an acceptance of professional power, is when the client sees his role as quite different and distinct from that of the professional. If, for example, the patient sees himself as having a clear responsibility for his own health he is unlikely to become dependent on the medical profession or to be ready to give unqualified acceptance to his doctor's nostrums. Robinson quotes evidence that in relation to their children's education middle-class mothers see far less of a distinction between their role and the role of the teacher. They are therefore less ready - in comparison with working-class mothers - to accept the traditional role of the client and to show deference towards, and acceptance of, professional authority (Robinson, 1978, p. 56).

Consumers do complain and protest about the exercise of professional power - increasingly so in recent years - but in many areas it is complaint within a context of acceptance; it is mute and passive rather than active and organised. Patients pocket their prescriptions but do not present them, or they present them but do not swallow the pills. Parents complain as they gather at the school gate about what is done or not done inside, but soon the children are old enough to go to school on their own, the parents no longer meet so regularly. Parent-teacher meetings and open days are too formal and forbidding occasions for the complaints that really concern parents to be voiced.

Underneath there is a deference to expertise and experience. In part it is genuine, in part it is the product of a realistic strategic appreciation of how the cards are stacked. A strategic position in the delivery of key services produces power and power produces acceptance - because there is little or no alternative.

To seek to generalise about the basis of professional power is to assume that there is such a phenomenon with a measure of unity about it. That assumption is valid in some measure. Clearly, different 'professions' have different characteristics, different degrees of expertise and mystery and perform very different tasks with very different clients. What this chapter has attempted is a general analysis of some of the factors which underpin the powers examined in the previous chapter. All the factors are significant at some times for all professions, established and aspirant, but not to the same degree.

4
The critique of professional power

In recent years the professions and the powers they wield have become the object of critical discussion. In part, the discussion is one aspect of the general challenge to existing status relationships which developed in the 1960s. Caplow has pointed out that in those years 'practically all non economic status relationships were challenged and extensively modified, ... relationships (in the USA at least) between whites and blacks, men and women, parents and children, teachers and pupils, consumers and producers' (Gartner and Riessman, 1974, p. 11). Everett Hughes has also suggested a link between general social unrest and criticism of the professions. 'Social unrest', he wrote, 'shows itself precisely in questioning of the prerogatives of the leading professions. In time of crisis, there may arise a general demand for more complete conformity of professionals to lay modes of thought, discourse and action' (1958, p. 83).

There are other reasons too why professional power is being challenged. Professionals have become scapegoats for their failure to transcend the limits imposed on them by shortage of resources. They have become the object of attack, for example, from the defenders of civil liberties for the immense and seemingly arbitrary power they wield over people, for an approach to clinical freedom which makes effective planning of resource use in the NHS so much more difficult, and for disregarding the concerns of their clients.

Inevitably the professions have suffered from the chill winds stirred up by the rise of consumerism and the calls from a more educated and articulate population for greater participation and professional accountability. Knowledge of quite different approaches to the staffing of supposedly professional services in other countries has led to questioning of the skills involved and the training required for professional work. There is also the critique posed explicitly and implicitly by the proliferation of self-help groups. 'While they differ greatly', Katz and Bender conclude, 'in the best self help groups there is an informality and accessibility, an openness that challenges the artificiality and self protective character of "professional" approaches in the human services' (1976, p. 239). There is also a record of proven effectiveness in widely different fields.

Finally the way in which almost all professionals have felt it necessary in recent years to take industrial action at the expense of their clients in pursuit of claims for higher wages or better conditions has damaged their public image.

The challenge to the position of the professions has been broad and has come from all parts of the political spectrum. The political left has asked whose side the professions are on. The political right has complained of monopoly and attacked the professions for pursuing policies which lacked public support. The utopians have attacked the professions as disabling people and creating dependency.

The critique is examined here under seven headings - that the professions have made excessive claims about the contribution they can make and have made to societal well-being; that they have been guilty of failures of responsibility; that their claim to political neutrality is a myth; that they trample on people's rights; that the service ideal has become tarnished; that the professions disable as well as enable; and that they are too often accountable to no one. What is being challenged are the claims which have always been taken for granted as justifications for the power which professionals wield.

I EXCESSIVE CLAIMS AND LIMITED ACHIEVEMENTS

A major element in the critique of the professions is that many of their claims to expertise are unsubstantiated or excessive and that their achievements are much more modest than their claims might lead the unbiased observer to expect. The importance of their contribution to the life of society and to the promotion of individual and social welfare is under attack.

There is now a substantial and growing body of literature

re-evaluating the role of the medical profession in the abolition of the great historic infectious diseases which have plagued mankind throughout history. 'At all stages of history', McKeown argues, 'doctors have overestimated the results of their intervention' (1971, p. 7). His thesis is that 'until the second quarter of the twentieth century the decline of mortality from infections owed little to specific measures of preventing and treating disease in the individual' (ibid., p. 32). Much more important were rising standards of living, better food supplies, increased concern with hygiene and reduction in family size. In ranking these influences McKeown concludes that effective prevention and treatment of disease in the individual 'have been less significant than any of the other major influences ... the health of men depends primarily on methods directed to populations rather than to individuals' (ibid., pp. 45, 48).

Powles argues a very similar case insisting, in contrast to the widespread belief that antibiotics and effective immunisation campaigns marked a break-through in the fight against infectious diseases, that 'their contribution to the total decline in mortality over the last two centuries has been a minor one' (1973, p. 6). The medical profession, then, has not by its own endeavours delivered the human race from past bondage to infectious disease.

What of its current contribution to human health and well-being? There is a mass of evidence which raises difficult questions about the contribution of health services to health. Maxwell, for example, in 'Health Care, The Growing Dilemma' points out that in any league table of the healthiness of populations in western countries, the United States comes near the bottom. And yet health expenditure per head of population in the USA is double or even treble that in other countries with seemingly better health records (Maxwell, 1975, p. 30). The Royal Commission on the National Health Service noted how Scotland with proportionally 50 per cent more hospital doctors and about 40 per cent more nurses and midwives than England had a lower life expectancy and a higher infant mortality rate (HMSO, 1979, para. 3.20). The point is a simple one - the key determinants of health are not health services. It has in the past generally and easily been assumed that they were, and this has contributed to the prestige of the medical profession and to governments' willingness to give the doctors what they wanted by way of resources. The realisation that their contribution to health is less significant than had been thought is one element in the emerging critique of the power and position of modern medicine. More specifically, Powles contrasts 'the enthusiasm associated with current developments and the reality of decreasing returns to health for rapidly increasing efforts' (1973, p. 1). Per capita expenditure on the NHS at constant prices has risen sharply since 1948 while at the same time - to take one limited index - the decline in mortality has tapered off almost to zero. Life expectancy at birth has hardly altered in the last generation, nor has life expectancy at age forty-five. Certainly, there have been slight gains in female life expectancy but the result is primarily to increase the number of lonely old widows, often poor, and increasingly handicapped.

The truth is that the diseases which are the scourge of industrial society are not, at the moment, susceptible to successful medical treatment. They are the diseases of maladaptation - heart disease and the cancers. They are not amenable to the engineering approach which dominates medicine. Enormous resources are invested in coronary care units, in screening for cancer, in cancer surgery. The outcome of such procedures is, at present, extremely dubious. National, regional and class differences in the incidence both of heart disease and cancer suggest very strongly that the causes are environmental, that the roots lie in particular ways of life. In principle, then, such diseases are preventable. If that is true, the role and contribution of the medical profession become less significant once it has pointed the way.

This changed pattern of disease, the failure of medicine to provide cures, together with the realisation that the best method of attack is often prevention in which the role of the medical profession can only be modest and indirect, all contribute to a potential lowering of the status of the medical profession. Medicine seems both less successful and less heroic apart from odd and exotic adventures such as transplant surgery.

These facts have certainly helped to fuel the critique of modern medicine. So too have a wide range of research findings of varied and inconsistent diagnosis, unnecessary hospitalisation, wide variations in hospital stay for similar conditions, the use of treatments proven to be inappropriate or ineffective, and wide regional variations in treatments, suggesting that the important factor is the idiosyncratic judgment of individual consultants rather than objective scientific truth. Reviewing the depressing volume of evidence on such issues Cooper comes to the melancholy conclusion that 'It is certain that much medical treatment is inappropriate, unproven or even unsound' (1975, p. 58; cf. Culyer, 1976; Cochrane, 1972).

The high claims - implicit and explicit - of the medical profession are a factor underlying doctor and patient dissatisfaction with the relationship in which they find themselves. The claims of the profession encourage people explicitly and implicitly to seek medical advice. One result of this is the large proportion of their consultations which GPs class as trivial or unnecessary. Williamson and Danaher, for example, estimate that probably a quarter of the physical conditions seen in general practice are those for which the doctor has no treatment other than that available to the patient (1978, p. 32; cf. Cartwright and Anderson, 1979). The fact that an estimated one third of patients do not use the drugs prescribed by their GP suggests a dissatisfaction with the outcome of the consultation and doubts about the GP's diagnosis or prescription. Similar doubts about some of the benefits of modern medicine are suggested by the dramatic drop in whooping cough vaccinations from 79 per cent of two-year-olds in 1972 to 38 per cent in 1976 as a product of anxieties about the risk of brain damage (ibid.). The evidence suggests a relationship between doctor, patient and modern medicine about which both parties have doubts.

My argument so far is a simple one. Firstly, recent research suggests that medicine's contribution to the elimination and control of infectious disease has been less important than most people, including the profession itself, have traditionally supposed. Secondly, traditional medicine's direct contribution to the elimination of the contemporary scourges of modern industrial society looks likely to be small. Thirdly, there are many questions to be answered about the way in which medicine is practised both by general practitioners and in hospitals. All raise doubts about the scientific nature of medicine, the skill and vigour with which it is often practised and its general state of health. As both evidence and expression of these doubts a new term - iatrogenic disease - has entered the language to describe the diseases produced by medical intervention.

Social workers are also open to this broad criticism of excessive claims and limited achievements. In some degree they have been used as the scapegoats for inadequate services, but they have not emerged unscathed from recent scandals - certainly their public standing has suffered. In

1965 Titmuss noted that 'during the last 20 years, whenever the British people have identified and investigated a social problem there has followed a national call for more social work and more trained social workers' (1968, p. 85). Such a call would be unlikely today. Social workers have claimed much and, as far as general public and policy makers can see, they have delivered comparatively little.

Social workers may not be to blame for the succession of child-care tragedies of recent years but most of the subsequent inquiries produced critical comments on the part social workers had played, or not played, in the events. Implicitly, if not explicitly, social workers had claimed to be able to prevent or deal with such situations - through more and longer training, through reorganisation of services into social services departments, through expansion in their numbers. Writing of the Maria Colwell case, Fitzherbert points out that, 'Taken together, more than enough people had more than enough knowledge and legal power to save her life' (1977, p. 171). In the case of fourteen-month-old Malcolm Page the family had been receiving intensive support from social worker and health visitor for eight months before he died ('Community Care', 24 January 1980). Many of those involved in the tragedy cases were criticised for poor communication, bad procedures and errors of professional judgment (ibid., 15 November 1979). To what extent criticisms of social service staff were legitimate is not the issue here. The issue is the damage done to the standing of the caring professions, social work in particular, and to their claims to possess and to be able to use expertise.

The British Association of Social Workers has recently argued that social workers should have an independent role which complements the medical role in compulsory admissions to mental hospitals. The Association stresses the essential part which the social worker plays in the decisions to invoke compulsory procedures. Bean's (1980) verdict, on the other hand, based on his empirical work on compulsory admissions was that 'social workers have no expertise which qualifies them to do anything except the most simple and basic tasks in the compulsory admission procedures'. There is other evidence too that social workers both feel and find themselves ill-equipped by training and experience for such work (Danbury, 1976, pp. 172-4). Fortunately, as Bean sees it, the body reviewing the Mental Health Act 1959 rejected BASW's 'ill-considered attempt to enlarge the legal power of social workers' (1979, p. 105) which is perhaps a sign of increasing scepticism about professional claims in general, and the claims of social workers in this particular area. Perhaps someone on the review body remembered Titmuss's sharp but gentle comment that 'Most professions, including the doctors and the lawyers, may sometimes be regarded as associations for spreading the gospel of self importance' (1968, p. 85).

What is at issue here with social work, as with medicine, is the validity and reliability of the knowledge base which is claimed. Does the profession really know how to deal with the ills which are its focus? Is the knowledge it uses scientific, valid and reliable? Do its treatments work? Is there a genuine corpus of professional knowledge about individual and social functioning which provides a basis for social work intervention on established lines of proven efficacy?

In relation to social work there are doubts both about the knowledge base which is claimed and about the use to which it can be put in the real world (Goldberg and Warburton, 1979, p. 2). Perhaps the crucial question is whether or not social workers feel themselves to have a corpus of knowledge on which they draw. From a wide-ranging examination of social work activities, Elizabeth Browne concluded that 'there was evidence that social workers used concepts from sociology, social and individual psychology to understand clients and their difficulties. But there was less evidence that these concepts had been assimilated into an integral system to guide practice' (HMSO, 1978c, p. 135). Another recent study asked a large sample of Local Authority social workers and probation officers which factors they felt contributed most to effectiveness in their work. Only 10 per cent of each group felt their professional skills and experience were the most helpful factor, compared with 30 per cent of Local Authority social workers and 39 per cent of probation officers who felt personal factors were most helpful (Holme and Maizels, 1978, pp. 58-9). The British Association of Social Workers has also argued that the key resource possessed by social workers 'is the social workers themselves' (ibid., p. 59). That may be true; if it is, what of the claim to knowledge and expertise as validating the professional claim?

If we look, for example, at an area of work where social work judgments are potentially extremely influential - the preparation of social inquiry reports - what we see is impressionistic rather than scientific documents. As Bean has pointed out, reports rarely contain information on factors which are known to be good predictors of criminality - for example age at first conviction or the number of previous convictions. Much more attention is devoted to factors of little predictive value. The crucial test of the scientific nature of the exercise is the reliability of the report - that is, if someone else collected information on the same issues, would it be the same. An examination of the reliability of information, Bean says, would reveal 'a number of profound and terrible truths' (1976, pp. 102-3).

The professional group which has perhaps been most publicly and generally pilloried for its excessive claims to expertise and its limited achievement is town planners. 'In many of the subjects (and they are legion)', writes Jon Gower Davies, 'on which planners pronounce, there is simply no such thing as an objective body of knowledge allied to a coherent theory which can be used as a basis for rational decision making' (1972, p. 222). Their successes are unobtrusive and forgotten, their failures are immortalised in bricks and concrete for all to see. In the 1940s and 1950s planners convinced local and central government that they had the skills to build the new Jerusalem not only in green and pleasant land but also in downtown urban Britain. Sometimes they succeeded, often they failed, and their failures became expensive and uninhabitable, the focus of a bitterness between service users and providers which invaded no other area of social policy. The planners' work did not just affect parts of the lives of individuals; it affected the whole way of life of whole communities. From the mid-1960s the supposed expertise of planners has increasingly been criticised as no more than value-laden opinion. Their ability to provide the framework for a fuller and more satisfying life has been sharply questioned and their failures have been publicised and condemned.

Teachers are open to the same kind of criticisms. Great claims have been made that there was an ample economic and social return to be reaped from increased expenditure on education. Experience leads to a sceptical view of such claims. Much, too, has been claimed for modern methods of education but never has there been such widespread concern about illiteracy among school leavers. The teachers argue continuously for smaller classes but there is no evidence that smaller classes lead to any improvement in pupil achievement. Similarly the extension of teacher training from two years to three years and the proliferation of four-year Bachelor of Education courses have not led to any clear educational benefits for the consumers of educational services. The belief which has nourished educational development in the post-war years, that more education was self evidently a mark of progress, is no longer unchallenged.

The medical profession still performs what to the layman are little less than miracles. The achievements of medicine are still more obvious than its excessive claims or its failures in competence. This is not so for social workers, for planners or for teachers. Their achievements are less obvious, less obviously miraculous and so do not balance their visible failures and the limited nature of the expertise on which they rely. But, whether at an academic or a more popular level, the skills, claims and achievements of the professions are less readily accepted as self evident than in the past and therefore form a less assured basis for the power the professions wield.

II FAILURES OF RESPONSIBILITY

'Failures of professional responsibility' is a useful heading under which various criticisms of the professions can be subsumed. The claim for professional status is based on the nature of certain tasks, the expertise involved in dealing with them, and the manner and spirit in which, it is claimed, they are conducted. In the last decade, the professions have come in for considerable criticism from researchers, government, the media and popular opinion for a range of alleged failures of professional responsibility.

There have been the scandals - essentially of two kinds, scandals to do with the running of long-stay institutions for the mentally ill and the mentally handicapped and scandals to do with the deaths of children for whom the Local Authority was responsible. In all these cases the actions and standard of work of professional staff have received rigorous examination and sharp criticism.

In the inquiry at Ely Hospital (HMSO, 1969a), a major share of responsibility for the situation which the Inquiry uncovered was laid at the door of the doctors in charge. The Physician Superintendent was judged to have had 'an insufficient appreciation of his necessary role as a spur to the improvement of conditions and as a potential champion of Ely' (ibid., para. 389). It was his duty, the Inquiry found, 'to say to the Hospital Management Committee over and over again, that the conditions prevailing at the hospital were unsatisfactory' (ibid.). This he did not do.

The same failures of professional responsibility emerge in varying degrees from the other inquiries. What is, however, even more striking is that conditions in long-stay hospitals were only revealed as a result of scandals. The medical profession played no part in bringing to public notice conditions which should have shocked professional opinion as sharply as they shocked public opinion. Any physician superintendent with a due and proper sense of his independent professional responsibility should have been besieging his Hospital Management Committee or Regional Hospital Board with a brutally factual report on prevailing conditions. If no satisfaction was forthcoming, professional ethics should surely have led him to take his concerns to Members of Parliament, the Secretary of State for Social Services, the columns of the popular press or the television studios. Those responsible for conditions in long-stay hospitals failed to assume the corollary of professional responsibility, which is the political responsibility to press for the resources required to deliver a professionally acceptable service. In the long-stay hospitals the professions lamentably failed in this responsibility. In fact, none of the great social welfare scandals of the 1960s - conditions in long-stay hospitals, the rediscovery of poverty, the slum school, homelessness, the conditions in old people's homes - were publicised by the responsible professionals. All had to await scandals or the work of researchers operating from so-called ivory towers. This must surely count as a major failure of professional responsibility.

Such failures are not accidental. They are the product of a particular orientation to work - professionalism - and the tunnel vision of professional responsibility and life in general to which it leads. Writing of the counsellor, Halmos says 'The large tasks, the issues of the great society, are not within his professional scope, and it is quite natural that both in training and in subsequent practice he will inadvertently transfer his curiosities, his excitements, and his sense of usefulness from the impersonal world of social reform to the intimate world of social therapy' (Halmos, 1965, p. 16). Larson's judgment is more general that 'the ideology of professionalism deflects the comprehensive and critical vision of society which is necessary to reassess the social functions of the profession' (1977, p. 237). Professionalism induces a narrowness of vision which leads inevitably to failures of responsibility.

In the wake of the cuts in public expenditure on education in the summer of 1979 head teachers decided to launch what the 'Guardian' (11 July 1979) described as 'an unprecedented campaign to inform parents of what the Government's public expenditure cuts mean for individual schools'. It was unprecedented because teachers have not in the past actively concerned themselves with issues of education resources. They have complained, but seldom taken any overt political action. Teachers could have eliminated many of the material disadvantages under which the education system groans, by giving government due and proper notice that, after an appropriate interval of say three, five or seven years, they would not teach in schools with overlarge classes, inadequate buildings, antique text books and all the other burdens produced by inadequate public expenditure. That would have been a professional use of power which would surely have produced widespread public support - and government action. Other professions could have pursued precisely similar and civilised professional campaigns on behalf of their clients. The professions have all campaigned on their own behalf, seldom for the services in which they work or on other relevant social issues. That is to fail an important test of professional responsibility.

In the child care scandals, the issues were rather less clear. But what emerged again and again in the inquiries was that well-meaning professionals failed in some way, even if for valid reasons, effectively to carry out their professional responsibilities. They failed to visit, they failed to liaise, they failed to coordinate, they failed to assert their legal rights to inspect and examine, they failed their clients, the public and themselves. Maybe the tasks they had assumed were impossible without more resources and round-the-clock surveillance of parents and children at risk, but the immediate reason for many of the tragedies was failure to perform duties according to what might be called professional standards.

Another failure of responsibility with which the professions can reasonably be charged is failure in self evaluation. The professions insist that the only acceptable form of evaluation is by other professionals who have insight into the 'arcana arcanorum' of professional skills. Even if such special pleading is accepted, the sad truth is that the professionals show scarcely more enthusiasm for professional evaluation than they do for evaluation by the prejudiced and ignorant laity. Dollery's (1971) suggestion for an Audit of

Health Care fell on stoney ground. 'We do not know', Horrobin writes of doctoring, 'whether most of the things which we do to patients are better for the welfare of that patient than if we had done nothing at all. And on the whole most of us prefer to remain warmly ignorant rather than coldly knowledgeable about the situation' (1978, p. 91).

The same dislike of evaluation is apparent in social work's failure to submit innovations in practice or organisation to monitoring or assessment. Such a task is complex but it would seem no more than responsible common sense to monitor new methods of social work, social work training and personal social services organisation and to attempt to evaluate the pros and cons of alternative approaches before sweeping changes are introduced. It would also seem wise to seek to evaluate current activities, but nowhere in their study of social work activities in thirty-one areas did the researchers in 'Social Service Teams' find departments or social workers who were subjecting any part of their direct work with clients to empirical testing (HMSO, 1978c, p. 136). Byrne makes a very similar point about educationists when she comments on their 'decidedly uneasy attitude towards, not to say rejection of, the concept of monitoring' (1976, p. 10). Such critical self examination, or self exposure to examination by others, seems alien to the aspiring - or arrived - professional. He asks to be taken in trust and faith - or hope. A mature, responsible professionalism must surely be self critical, ready to evaluate and to be evaluated in the interests of professional and scientific development.

Another issue of considerable public concern where the medical profession as such has failed to assume any responsibility for evaluating the quality of service is in relation to commercial deputising services. There is clear evidence that some doctors are making excessive use of such services. There is also anxiety - which the BMA shares - about the quality of some services, but the BMA has had nothing to say about the standard of services and has shown no commitment to control those bringing such services into disrepute ('Guardian', 6 December 1978).

As well as a dislike of evaluation, the professions also display a reluctance to take account of published research findings. All professions claim a scientific base of some kind for their practice. An important element in such a claim is the willingness to re-examine practice, to be open to new knowledge, to alter what one does in the light of research. The medical profession has shown a great reluctance to take account of research on a wide range of issues - the optimum length of hospital stays, the ineffectiveness of certain treatments and prescriptions, for example. Teachers, equally, have responded with reluctance to the now well-established research findings on the importance of parental involvement in education to children's achievement. No teacher would knowingly do things in the classroom which were calculated to impede a child's educational development. What is being done in the ignoring of the research findings on the educational benefits of parental involvement is just as detrimental to the child's educational development as depriving him or her of more obviously educational activities in the classroom. Such action needs to be regarded as equally lacking in professional responsibility.

Another charge levelled against the professions in relation to professional responsibility is that the struggle for professionalism gives a wrong focus to the service and activity which the profession is pursuing. Some critics would argue that this has happened to social work. In a search for professional status, social work has emphasised a medical, psychotherapeutic, individualised model of work because that seemed the best way of asserting its expertise and professionalism. This substantially closed off other kinds of valuable and socially necessary activities - or at best led social workers to regard them as of less than primary importance in their work. In the same way, the medical profession's questionable focus on the individual patient rather than on societal programmes for better health is the legacy of historical patterns of practice which conferred status and the accolade of professionalism on practice with individuals.

The argument is that the struggle for professional status leads to a concentration on a particular kind of work with individuals which leads to a narrow view of the professional task, and a neglect of what are equally proper professional responsibilities. It also leads to an emphasis that the professional responsibility is to individuals rather than to society as a whole, and is extrapolated by the medical profession to the tendentious level of arguing that because the doctor is accountable in an ethical and legal sense to the patient, he cannot therefore be accountable in any other sense to a managerial body.

The professional does have to balance and reconcile various conflicts of responsibility and interest - to the client, to the public, to his profession. 'Perhaps the least satisfactory reconciliation' suggests MacIver, 'is that relating the interest of the client to the interest of the public, not merely in the consideration of the particular cases as they arise but still more in the adaptation of the service to the needs of the public as a whole as distinct from those of the individual clients' (Vollmer and Mills, 1966, p. 54). It is part of the professional responsibility to struggle with this reconciliation, not to ignore the issues it raises. To assert responsibility to individuals as the only professional responsibility - which is what clinical freedom so often amounts to - is to be socially irresponsible and to neglect the interests of all other clients except the one currently being treated.

What is at issue in the tension between professional responsibilities to individuals and to society is the breadth or narrowness of the focus of professional activity. This is important at another level as well - the level of service organisation. Services organised around professional skills are a tribute to the power of professionals in policy making. They also bear witness to a failure of professional responsibility. This is a failure to recognise that services organised around particular skills may be logical for professionals but may not meet the needs of clients and potential clients. The real sufferers for example, from the multiplicity of professionals actually or potentially involved in the care and rehabilitation of the physically handicapped are the handicapped. When professionals cannot - or do not - resolve their rivalries and status problems in order to work in services which are client, rather than profession, oriented that too is a failure of responsibility.

How is such narrowness of focus to be explained? Very relevant is the whole process of professional socialisation. A main aim of that process is the building of a professional identity. The result is to make the profession rather than the client the professional's prime focus and concern. He becomes profession- rather than client-oriented, showing his professionalism through identification with professional concerns, values and interests rather than client needs. Training in isolation from other students - which is the general pattern of professional training - also generates in the profession what Freidson calls 'a self deceiving view of the objectivity and reliability of its knowledge and of the virtues of its members' (1970b, pp. 369-70). This contributes to the narrow focus of the profession, the reluctance professionals often show to cooperate with colleagues from other professions, and their overweening confidence in their judgment on a wide range of issues often only tenuously connected with their central concerns.

Finally, there is the charge that the professions lack responsibility in that they do not look long or closely enough at the overall impact of their activities particularly on vulnerable groups. Simmie makes this point very effectively about town planning. 'If town planning is to claim', he writes, 'that it represents an altruistic, neutral and rational agency mediating on behalf of the public interest, it is necessary to be both explicit and accurate about which groups benefit and which groups lose by virtue of its activities' (Simmie, 1974, pp. 131-2). Social workers have not looked very closely at the implications for their clients of the unification of personal social services into one monopolistic, centralised bureaucracy. Doctors equally are open to the charge that they have given inadequate thought to how developments in general practice or in hospital organisation have affected the most vulnerable among their patients. There is much to be said for the view that developments have been to the disadvantage of those whose needs are greatest.

In a range of different areas, and for a variety of different reasons the welfare professions' sense of responsibility has come under critical examination in recent years. They have taken a substantial amount of blame, deserved and undeserved, for the welfare scandals and tragedies of recent years. Their sense of responsibility has, at times, been narrow to the point of myopia. They have not seen it as a corollary of their responsibility to individuals to pursue the needs of services through political action. They have been reluctant to encourage or even allow evaluation of their work and to take note of its findings. Because of particular biases the professions have given inadequate attention to certain needs groups. The critique of the professions' sense of responsibility is compelling.

III THE CLAIM FOR NEUTRALITY

A major plank in the professional assertion is that the professions are only concerned with service to individuals. Their work, it is claimed, has nothing to do with politics and the reverberating contemporary issues of justice and equality. Guided by certain values acceptable to all men of good will, what they do is of benefit to all.

The professions have in recent years been exposed to the question 'Whose side are you on?' The sharp criticism of structural-functional sociology and its consensus model of society, and the re-assertion of the political element in the work of even the most apolitical seeming groups has opened up the work of the professions to fresh analysis. The whole notion of the national interest, of political neutrality, and of the inevitable beneficence of work focused on, and ending with, individuals, has been challenged.

Service to individuals, in the pan-political model of social ills, is, almost by definition, conservative in its implications, because work with individuals does nothing about 'the system' and is therefore symptom-oriented. It stops short of dealing with causes. It is certainly beyond dispute that most professional work is with individuals and this means that the causes of problems - ill health, educational failure, delinquency, mental illness - are not tackled. In the past, the causes were defined as being individual rather than systemic. The individual and society both benefited from their resolution. When such problems come to be seen as substantially or inherently structural, then action directed towards individuals comes to be seen as ineffective and, in so far as it does alleviate problems, it is supportive of the very system which causes them.

The professional focus on individuals implies a taken-for-granted notion of the issues. Such a diagnosis specifies the areas of skill which are the expertise of the professional - dealing with ill people, educating individual children, seeking to increase self knowledge in the deviant. The professions developed on the basis of work with individuals. That was where problems became manifest, that was where they were located, that was clearly, so it seemed, where action was required. Such an approach does close off other approaches. It takes the politics out of social - and individual - problems. If it does this, it cannot be a politically neutral activity. To regard social problems as individual and unpolitical, or at least to act as though they were, is to collude with the existing social and economic order, to side with those whose interests are firmly rooted in the continuance of the status quo. Professional work cannot then be regarded as neutral. Its focus is either an implicit statement about causation or an implicit statement in support of the existing economic and social structure which produces the situations with which the profession deals. If the fundamental characteristic of society is conflict of interests rather than consensus, then there are no neutrals. Neutrality is a delusion. All positions are political stances.

Titmuss raised questions about professional neutrality and the distribution of social services more than fifteen years ago. He stressed the significance of the middle-class background of most professional groups and their absence of contact with working-class culture. 'Thus', he argued,

> they bring to their work middle class values in the processes of giving or withholding medical care, education, legal aid and welfare benefits. Their model of the ideal pupil, student, patient and client is one with middle class values and a middle class tongue. This process, subtle and often unconscious, partly explains why in Britain, under universally available welfare services, the middle classes tend to receive better services and more opportunities for advancement.... Of all professions in contact with the poor, only social workers in their training learn to understand the significance of this factor in their relationships. They recognise the importance of guarding professionalism against functioning as a disequalizing force (Titmuss, 1965, p. 364).

Medicine's concentration on the individual as the proper target for medical intervention looks like a completely neutral stance but the result is to leave the health-denying properties of our society off the agenda. One of the elements in Illich's critique of modern medicine is that it functions to preserve a way of life which is health-denying. It does this, by making it rather less intolerable than it would otherwise be, through the liberal prescription of, for example, sleeping tablets and antidepressants (Illich, 1975).

One of the most striking health statistics is that infant mortality rates in social class V are double those in social class I. The gap remains today the same as it was thirty years ago. One reason for the absence of change is the medical profession's focus on individuals and its failure to impress on successive governments the significant determinants of infant death rates. The profession has defined the matter as one of the health of individuals and has sought to do what it could by action at that level. It has taken no major recent initiatives to raise the basic social inequalities which continue to be a crucial cause of this holocaust. To deal with health at the individual level only, is implicitly to accept tight limitations on what can be done. It may be a professional decision, but it is also a political act. It is not neutral; it helps to underpin a system of distribution of opportunities and disabilities which is profoundly unequal - and health- and life-denying.

Till comparatively recently the influence of teachers on the distribution of educational opportunity has not been much studied. The effect of classifying children has certainly been shown to affect their subsequent performance. Teachers' expectations, too, are known to be an important influence on children's educational development. Recent research by Rutter (1979), Power (1967), Reynolds (1976) and others shows that the nature of the school does make a substantial difference to children's educational performance. How the school is organised, staff attitudes to the pupils and their degree of concern for them, the nature of the academic emphasis of the school, the system of rewards and punishments, have all been shown to be important to educational outcomes. The preconceptions and beliefs which teachers bring to their work and the way in which they define issues of equality of opportunity are critical to educational outcomes. It is not an activity carried on in some kind of politically and morally neutral vacuum.

Professional neutrality has been attacked from another perspective too. Talk of treatment for delinquency, it is argued by some, is simply to use euphemistic talk to disguise the fact of coercion. Treatment and cure are terms suggesting the primacy of the client's interests. He is the supposed focus. Society is providing a service for his benefit. In fact, it is society's needs not the child's or young person's which demand that action be taken to combat anti-social behaviour. Talk of treatment is thus to describe in technical terms an act which is political - an act undertaken against an individual for the good of the majority. It removes or reduces moral, social, and political conflicts in society if such difficult and diverse issues can successfully be defined as technical and professional and the vital decisions be handed over to the professions.

Historically, it has been a source of strength to the professions that they could be regarded as neutral in the conflicts of economic, social and political life. That neutrality has been powerfully challenged, by the radical sociology of the 1960s and, more specifically, by studies of the impact and implications of particular patterns of professional practice or action. Given the tearing down of the veil of neutrality, the work of the professions has to be assessed on new and broader criteria. If an increasing range of professional activity can truly and fairly be defined as political in its effect on the distribution of goods, services and opportunities, and its effect on people's rights as individuals - then it must be judged in that light. When that is done, the professions' contribution to a more just and equitable society is undistinguished.

If professional activity is expert, politically neutral and for the general good, it can claim the support of all men of goodwill. Once it comes to be seen as political, the supportive consensus cracks. Power and privilege which are accepted and acceptable if exercised for the general good become open again to debate and criticism once they are recognised as having political effects as in the distribution of rights, opportunities and socially valued goods and services. The effects of professional action become both an element in the critique of the professions and a stimulus to a broader re-examination of professional power and privilege. Political neutrality can justify power. When that neutrality is questioned, questioning of the power follows.

IV NEGLECT OF RIGHTS

One of the charges pressed vigorously against the professions in recent years is that they trample on people's basic rights as citizens. There are three areas of work where the charge is pressed with particular vigour - in the field of mental health, in the field of child care and delinquency, and in the broader area of the provision of information to clients and users of services.

At the root of the power and discretion of the professionals in the first two areas is a medical model of mental illness or delinquency. A medical model means that the professional defines the problem. Only he, and not the client, knows what the problem really is. Only he, therefore, can prescribe for it. The adoption of a treatment model in dealing with delinquents means, furthermore, that what is done is for the good of the offender. These two elements in the situation - the power which belongs to the professional to define the situation, and the fact that what is being done has as its primary and sole concern the good of the person being treated, mean that to erect barriers or safeguards against independent professional action is to present obstacles to his doing good to whomever needs his services.

The critical response to this approach has three main

strands. A growing number of commentators have begun to ask whether what is provided for the mentally ill, or for delinquents under the label of 'treatment', is, in fact, for their good. On a rather crude 'the end justifies the means' approach, what might be acceptable if it works becomes open to debate if it does not.

Secondly, writers have begun to ask about the nature of the decision involved when people are deprived of liberty. Lieberman argues that decisions about what does or does not justify restrictions on liberty or incarceration are political and that policy makers have been deluded in classifying such decisions as medical or professional (1970, p. 213). Szasz has made the same point insisting that 'depriving a person of his liberty is a moral and political act' (Bean, 1976).

Thirdly, professional power over people has been set squarely in the context of arguments about democracy and social rights. Lieberman (1970, p. 7) expresses this point of view in his statement that 'inherent in the meaning of professionalism and the motives of its adherents is the negation of democracy itself, stemming from the incipient belief that the citizen, like the consumer, is incompetent to make important decisions affecting his life.' This concern is fed and fuelled by the revived concern about rights in a more centralised, more bureaucratised and more computerised society. Freidson is making this point - which ties in with the first point made earlier - when he writes 'Short of immediate threats to life itself, the civil dignity of the layman is, I believe, a far more important element of his welfare than much of what the [medical] profession, dominated by its own occupational perspective, would call his health' (1970b, pp. 354-5).

Let us look briefly at the assertion that in the field of mental health the professionals trample on people's rights. We have looked earlier at the considerable powers of the professionals under the Act which, in Kathleen Jones's words, 'freed practitioners and patients from the shackles of a highly legalistic system' (1977). What for one commentator, of course, is freedom from legal shackles is, to another, deprivation of vital legal safeguards. The vagueness of the definitions of mental disorder says Hoggett 'compares unfavourably with the statutory definitions of most criminal offences' (1976, p. 56). The result is to put considerable power in the hands of the professionals to interpret the law as they act upon it. Only the professionals define mental illness and the courts have generally been reluctant to challenge professional decisions (R. Jones, 1978).

The Mental Health Act 1959 also gives those working with the mentally ill very great protection from legal action by patients. Section 141 of the Act, for example, provides that no one can be liable for any act purporting to be done in pursuance of the Mental Health Act unless the act was done in bad faith or without reasonable care. Furthermore, anyone wishing to pursue a grievance under Section 141 has first of all to seek the leave of the High Court. The High Court will not give leave for the action to proceed unless satisfied that there is a substantial ground for the contention that the person to be proceeded against acted in bad faith or without reasonable care. It might be argued that the professions have here a degree of protection which is unnecessary, improper, and a denial of the basic rights of complainants to have their case examined without undue delay, cost, or procedural difficulty.

While appeal against a compulsory admission order can only be lodged after a patient has been admitted, there is no statutory duty laid on the hospital - or on anyone else - to provide the information that there is such an avenue of appeal. That would seem to contravene a basic right, as does the fact that the appellant may well lack full knowledge of the case against him. Hoggett points out that in Mental Health Review Tribunals the hospital can make available to the Tribunal information which is never disclosed to the patient. The Tribunal may decide that the information should be so disclosed, but it may be that the patient is never given the opportunity to combat allegations against him because no one has told him what those allegations are (Hoggett, 1976, p. 154).

The 1959 Act deliberately set out to free professionals to be professional. In that endeavour the rights of patients were placed in second place. One reason was dislike of the restraints imposed by a legalistic approach. Another was the medicalisation of mental illness and the attempt to assimilate practices to those for dealing with physical illness. A third was optimism about the future achievements of the medical profession in the treatment of mental illness. Twenty years on, opinion on all these three points has moved against the professions.

Another area of concern about the impact of professional power on the rights of the individual is the field of child care and the treatment of delinquency. The notion that what the delinquent needs is treatment rather than punishment has wide-ranging implications for the power and role of the professional - and the rights of the offender. If the delinquent requires treatment, it needs to be individualised to deal with his particular social sickness. The role of the court must, of necessity, be diminished because its concern is with justice rather than treatment and it lacks expertise. The power of the professional is therefore increased. Furthermore, if the delinquent is in some sense 'sick', his or her act of delinquency must be regarded as no more than a symptom of the real, underlying malaise. Such a view means that the delinquent has few rights. He cannot claim that his act of delinquency was trivial and that his 'treatment' should therefore be brief and simple. Also, if he is in some measure sick, he can have no responsibility for his acts save to get cured as soon as possible and that can only mean accepting and following the professional prescription.

A legal approach is usually accompanied by procedural rules designed to safeguard the position of the accused. In the juvenile court these are widely neglected in the interests of the supposed welfare of the offender - and at the expense of his rights. Some juvenile courts, for example, deny parents and children access to school and social inquiry reports - and so the opportunity to challenge and refute them. Such reports can also contain hearsay evidence of a kind which would be totally inadmissible in an ordinary court of law ('Guardian', letter, 31 March 1976).

The whole professional ideology of treatment militates against a concern for rights. We know little, says Parsloe, about how social workers and probation officers use their discretion at court hearings, 'What we do know suggests that they are little concerned about clients' "rights"' (Parsloe, 1978, p. 241). The social worker's all-embracing role as diagnostician, prescriber, treatment executant, sanctioner in the case of non compliance, and befriender also gives grounds for concern. Such a concentration of power and responsibility in one person is as unhealthy, and as considerable a threat to liberty, as is the failure to guarantee the separation of powers in the body politic.

Reporting before the therapeutic deluge had washed through the corridors of power, the Ingleby Committee recorded its view that 'Residence in an approved school involves considerations affecting the liberty of the subject, and we think it important that a decision to commit a child to an approved school should be taken by a judicial body'

(HMSO, 1960, para. 341). Such considerations have been rejected because of an ideology which has its roots in confidence in professional judgment. Concern about the quality of the latter helps feed doubts and anxieties about the former and its implications. So too does a more abstract concern for rights. Together they contribute to anxiety about professional power and children's rights.

Finally, there is the issue of the rights of clients, patients and users of services to information about their condition and their treatment. The issue is at its sharpest in relation to the securing of genuinely informed consent to hazardous or irreversible surgical procedures and courses of medical treatment, particularly when the patient is unable readily to understand what is involved. But the matter is more generally important than that. What is at issue is the fundamental attitude of professions - in this particular case the medical profession - towards clients. Freidson suggests that the whole pattern of admission and treatment to hospital is based on the premise that 'the patient is incompetent to judge what is needed and in order to be cured must put himself passively into the hands of the staff, obeying them without question and allowing them to do to him what they see fit' (1970b, p. 133). The attitude to the right of patients to information depends on attitudes towards the broader issue of professional-patient relationships and the role of the patient. There is now good evidence to suggest that the provision of full information to patients can lead to earlier discharge from hospital and recovery, so it is not just an abstract issue of rights (Cox and Mead, 1975, p. 225).

Because of the professional medical mystique patients are slow to ask for information or apologetic about asking. When information is supplied it is frequently not understood. Doctors and hospitals alike are poor at telling people what is wrong, what can or cannot be done about it, what the effect of drugs will be, for how long they must do or not do particular things and so on. Research for the Royal Commission on the NHS showed that 31 per cent of inpatients and 25 per cent of outpatients considered that they had not been given sufficient information about their treatment and progress (HMSO, 1979, para. 10.26). Very few hospitals supply patients with written material about the typical after effects and recovery period for common operations or illnesses. There is ample research evidence on the fallibility of verbal communication and on how little of what is said is understood or correctly remembered. The medical profession has taken little account of this - or of what is surely a basic human need and right - to know what is being done and why.

The right to information is not only an issue in medicine. Writing of the dissatisfactions of parents with handicapped children, Robinson's verdict was that 'Without much doubt the commonest complaints concern the quantity and quality of communications with the services and, especially, with the helping professionals themselves' (1978, p. 9). As the parents of one mentally handicapped child put it, 'We need to be taken into the confidence of those who have professional skills, not offered a few crumbs of information when someone else decides how much it is good for us to know' (ibid.). Norman Dennis argues the same case on behalf of the residents of Millfields in their dealings with the planners. 'A very high proportion of "technical" and "political" facts and factors which are "beyond the grasp of Millfields",' he suggests, 'are in reality perfectly comprehensible to any Millfield ten-year-old not in the bottom quarter of the intelligence distribution ...' (ibid., p. 24).

To fail to supply information, to fail to make sure it is available and comprehensible to the layman, is evidence of a particular view of professionalism. It is usually both dysfunctional to the task in hand and tramples on a basic right - but it remains widespread in the professional world. The last two decades have been years in which many new rights have been asserted and old ones reasserted. 'The right to know' has been insisted upon in a wide range of disparate areas of life. The professions have made some concessions to the movement - usually minimal and frequently reluctant.

V THE SERVICE IDEAL

As with other elements in the professional armoury the service ideal has been re-examined and re-evaluated in recent years. Such re-assessment has embraced two elements - examination of how professional associations and individual professionals actually behave or have behaved in particular situations and, secondly, consideration of the varied latent functions of the service ideal following the realisation that such ideals have functions over and above that of simply stating professional values.

Investigation of the behaviour of professional associations

and individual professionals, as might be expected, shows that they are not always motivated purely and simply by an ideal of service and that their behaviour does not always match their publicly stated codes of practice. The ethical code of the American Medical Association, for example, lays down that 'A profession has for its prime object the service it can render to humanity, reward or financial gain should be a subordinate consideration' (Vollmer and Mills, 1966, p. 51). In the behaviour of the Association in the recent past a concern for financial gain has been much more obvious to any but the most partial observer than any concern to serve humanity. Another indication that the medical profession is less than totally preoccupied with the needs of suffering humanity is the fact that every health system in the world, in industrial or developing, capitalist or socialist countries, finds it extremely difficult to get doctors to go to those areas where they are most needed.

In the United States the proliferation of malpractice suits against doctors is an indication that people are no longer prepared to take for granted either the doctor's competence or his commitment to his patients' interests. Such suits show and stimulate a lack of confidence in the profession and in its ideals. A wide range of factors underlie this decline in public confidence - some to do with social movements, consumerism for example, others to do with the medical profession's behaviour - its manifest concern to maximise its own financial rewards, for example or the scandal of the misuse of medicaid funds in New York City in the early period of the programme when an estimated one billion dollars was misappropriated by medical practitioners (O'Connor, 1973, pp. 164-5).

Another scandal of a quite different kind which struck at the very heart of professional claims to an ideal of service was the revelation that doctors in the USA had allowed dying cancer patients to be exposed to massive doses of radiation to analyse the psychological and physical results of simulated nuclear fall-out. In the end the experiments were stopped - but only after they had been going for eleven years (Cox and Mead, 1975, p. 183).

In Britain there have been no such dramatic blows to the belief in the service ethic of the professions but there has been a steady undermining and erosion of public faith. During the 1970s the major welfare professions all did things that would have been unthinkable in earlier decades. Hospital doctors worked to rule in pursuit of more money and a forty-hour week. For periods in 1975 and 1976 senior medical staff only treated emergency cases, because they objected to the decision of the government of the day to remove private beds from NHS hospitals. Several thousand social workers in some twenty areas went on strike in 1979, some for many months. Teachers have left children unattended at lunch time. Whether or not such actions were justified is a difficult question to answer. What was made very visible through the media, however, was professions who stress an ethic of service, pursuing industrial action which left their clients uncared for or with only skeletal services. The professional groups involved seemed no different from any other group of workers trying to win over-the-odds material gains.

The General Practitioner Charter Working Group Report of February 1979 ('BMJ', 24 February 1979) is an interesting statement of how certain GPs, at least, would like to reinterpret the profession's traditional ethic of service. In seeking a variety of supplementary payments for out-of-hours services and for additional services over and above what the Group regard as the normal pattern of GP responsibility, the BMA Group is seeking to redefine and limit the responsibility of the GP for his patients. His responsibility would no longer be to provide, as a normal service, for his patients' medical needs wherever those arose and whatever they were. The Report is a retreat from that traditional broad concept of professional service to a narrow more restricted approach to the GP's obligations with extra payment for services considered to be outside the normal bounds of duty.

There is a feeling, too, that many of the developments in general practice in recent years have not been entirely for the benefit of patients. Cartwright's most recent research on 'Patients and Their Doctors 1977' lends support to this view. She seeks to answer the question 'Who has really benefited from the recent changes in general practice - the doctor or the patient?' 'Many of our data', she concludes, 'suggest that a number of the changes - the increase in partnerships, in appointment systems, in ancillary help, in deputising services - have made working conditions more acceptable to GPs, but have not increased patients' satisfaction and have sometimes been detrimental to this' (Cartwright and Anderson, 1979). The evidence certainly suggests a weakening in the service orientation of the doctor. Some of the characteristics of medical practice which witnessed most clearly to the service ethic such as readiness to make home visits on request and twenty-four-hour-a-day emergency availability have become less obvious or have disappeared.

In social work there seems to be evidence of dissatisfaction among social workers in the field with the focus and politics of the dominant professional body, the British Association of Social Workers. In the mid-1970s, Phoebe Hall noted a reluctance among many younger social workers 'to join a professional body which they feel places the interests of the profession far higher than those of clients they are supposed to be helping' (1976, p. 130). The debate within social work about the desirability or otherwise of a Social Work Council to register social workers and take responsibility for standards of work provides evidence of the same concern among social workers that their professional leaders are in danger of getting their priorities wrong and forgetting their fundamental aims of care and service. 'The reason for pursuing the idea of a Social Work Council', one social worker wrote recently, 'is to increase the professional status, power and privileges of social workers' (Didrichsen, 1979).

Ours is a cynical society, less willing perhaps to accept protestations of altruism or to accept altruistic behaviour at its face value than people were in the past. We no longer expect people to be motivated solely or even primarily by a concern for service. In such an atmosphere the claims of the professions will be treated less respectfully than formerly. They will be examined with suspicion and scepticism. In such a situation, the professions have felt the need to adopt new and more militant methods to preserve their position in the hierarchy of pay and privilege - which make protestations of an ideal of service sound rather hollow. Outsiders and critics see the professions as using their clients, often the most helpless and needy in society, as counters in the struggle for a better deal for themselves.

Other experts add further grist to the mills of anti-professionalism. They point to the way in which the professions have only ill-developed codes of ethics covering their relationship to society as a whole. In the USA, for example, the medical profession has clearly neglected the interests and needs of the poor and the black population in its pursuit of issues alleged to be crucial to the freedom of medicine. In the UK the medical profession has connived at the neglect of services for certain of the most helpless groups in society. In the halcyon days of the 1950s and 1960s a significant proportion of the output of United Kingdom medical schools emigrated shortly after qualification after long and costly training at public expense in search of higher rewards and without regard to the shortages so created.

The point is simple. In the 1970s a range of factors, specific and general, led to a questioning of the ideal of service which the professions had always asserted as one of the major justifications for their status and position in society. If the justifications come to be regarded with less certainty, the position itself, becomes more open to attack.

VI DISABLING EFFECTS

A recent allegation about the effects of the professions is that they can render people less able to cope with the ordinary problems of day-to-day living in spite of the fact that their explicit aim and purpose is to improve people's ability to function independently. The argument is that while initially people become dependent on the professions for specialist skills and services, gradually they become dependent on them for services which, in the past, individual citizens performed for themselves or for each other. The effect on individuals and communities is to narrow their range of capacities and to 'disable' them.

Illich, of course, is the great protagonist of this point of view. 'I propose', he writes, 'to call the mid-twentieth century the Age of Disabling Professions' (1978, p. 39). Illich's critique contains a strong dash of romanticism but in it fantasy is spiced with realism. To what extent and in what ways do the welfare professions enable and disable people?

The school can provide an environment conducive to learning and teaching where both are undertaken in a purposeful, organised way. That is the traditional argument for professional education, that at certain stages and levels, education needs to be pursued in specialised institutions under professional guidance and direction. Illich puts the disabling view, attacking the school as an institution, and by implication, professional educators. 'The mere existence of school', he writes, 'discourages and disables the poor from taking control of their own learning. All over the world the school has an anti-educational effect on society: school is recognised as the institution which specialises in education. The failures of school are taken by most people as a proof that education is a very costly, very complex, always arcane and frequently almost impossible task' (1973a, p. 75). The points Illich is making about the disabling impact of professionalised education need to be drawn out. There are really three of them. First, the existence of specialised educational institutions - schools - means that people are discouraged from pursuing their own education. Secondly, because of the view that school is where education takes place, no effort is made to develop the educative possibilities of ordinary life. Thirdly, the failures of school, and indeed its very existence, suggest that education is a complex, very expensive and difficult activity. The educational process is mystified so discouraging all but the obtuse and the unreasonable from pursuing it except under professional guidance.

In the field of pre-school education many professional educators have been unenthusiastic about the non-professional play group movement stressing that education is essentially a professional task and discouraging non-professional developments. They have stressed the need for the extension of professionally provided nursery education. That can be regarded as a way of supplementing the skills and expertise of parents, of enabling them to be better parents and educators. On the other hand, the professionalisation of pre-school education can have quite opposite effects. In Lady Plowden's words 'The confidence of parents in themselves as parents, in this rapidly changing society, where the urgent need is for confidence and security, has been lessened. It is "they" in nurseries and schools who know best, from the earliest months and years of a child's life ...' (Land, 1978, p. 270).

There can be little doubt that professional educators disable some of those they seek to teach. By adopting a negative attitude to the child's background and experiences, by classifying children in such a way that the child's expectations of himself are limited or downgraded, by failing to encourage parental involvement in the educational process, children can be disabled educationally. Those who leave school at sixteen scarcely able to read and write have been disabled - or at best not enabled by the people and institutions designed to achieve those very aims. Paulo Freire has shown the potentialities for self education when a start is made from the position of the learner rather than that of the teacher (1972, ch. 1), but that is to challenge the teacher's professional judgment about method and technique.

Similar arguments are put forward about the professionalisation of health care. Illich expounds at length what he calls the 'health denying effects' of the health professions, by which he means the destruction of 'the potential of people to deal with their human weakness, vulnerability and uniqueness in a personal and autonomous way' (1975a, p. 26). Certainly, the medical profession has successfully medicalised whole areas of life. 'For Her Own Good: 150 years of Experts' Advice to Women' (Ehrenreich and English, 1979), for example, documents the gradual takeover of traditional female skills in health and child care by the professionals. Child birth has been thoroughly medicalised - and in recent years brought ever more completely under medical control by the increase in the proportion of births taking place in hospital. 'As professionally engineered delivery models [of childbirth] reach these independent women', Illich writes, 'the desire, competence, and conditions for autonomous behaviour are being destroyed' (1978, p. 11).

Illich's emphasis is on the dependence which follows from the professionalisation of health and on the damage which professionalism does to informal health care systems. People cease to feel the same responsibility for their own health, for its maintenance or for the treatment of minor ills. Traditional remedies are discarded in favour of professionally validated nostrums. The effects of professional medicine can also be destructive even for the practice of professional medicine. 'As medicine encroaches on more of human life', writes Carlson, 'it further incapacitates its major ally - the patient - from assuming responsibility for health. In so doing, it weakens its own capacities to heal' (1975, p. 46). The dependent disabled patient makes unnecessary demands on professional health services because he has been socialised to the view that only the doctor can be trusted to diagnose what is wrong with him and to put it right. He has also been schooled to the view that the doctor can put right almost everything that is wrong with him most conveniently and easily through the prescription of appropriate drugs. Professional medicine has helped to induce this reliance on drugs to produce health which increases the demand for and dependence on professional services.

Illich attacks professional health care with a flail. He ignores major achievements of scientific medicine. But he has drawn attention to important issues and there are many points in his critique which would be accepted by the health professionals. What they fail to see, however, is that the dependence and lack of self helpfulness about which they complain in their patients and clients are, in substantial measure, the product of the way they as professionals approach their work, seeing and asserting themselves as the experts with the answers.

Social workers, because their precise function is more obscure than that of teachers or doctors, are in some ways most exposed to the charge of rendering their clients incapable of standing fairly and firmly on their own two feet. They can easily be pilloried as the nursemaids of the nanny state. 'By their very existence', thundered the 'Daily Mail' in a blistering attack on social workers on 18 January 1980, 'they not only stop individuals doing things for themselves, they stop groups and communities doing things for their fellow citizens.'

The argument is that by freeing people from responsibilities which are rightly theirs - for dealing with difficult children, for coping with handicaps, for caring for dependants - people become less able to cope with other responsibilities which life brings; they lose an opportunity for growing into that autonomy which Illich values so highly. The second argument is that the availability of public help from social workers and social services deprives groups and communities of the incentive and the necessity to provide their own services. They become at the same time less able to help themselves and dependent on the help of others. Speaking of his own experience as a parent with a mentally handicapped child, and of his conclusions after interviewing other parents in the same situation, Hannan concluded that having things done for one 'helps at first; but in the long run it deprives one of the will to participate or to make constructive suggestions' (1975, p. 116). It breeds passivity and acceptance.

In another specific example Scott describes how the professional ideology of those seeking to help the handicapped cope with their disability can function to disable them because of the way in which it demands that they view themselves. The expert, he writes,

> has been specially trained to give professional help to impaired people. He cannot use his expertise if those who are sent to him for assistance do not regard themselves as being impaired. Given this fact, it is not surprising that the doctrine has emerged among experts that truly effective rehabilitation and adjustment can occur only after the client has squarely faced and accepted the 'fact' that he is, indeed, 'impaired' (Scott, 1970, p. 280).

The expert demands that the handicapped person sees himself as disabled as a prerequisite of being helped, but this can undermine his ability to help himself and to live a normal life.

Social work can have the same disabling effect on delinquents. The very notion of the delinquent as needing treatment implies that he is sick. Sickness is something for which one cannot be held responsible, so one cannot be held responsible for any delinquent acts. Such an attitude is an implicit attack on a person's concept of himself as a sentient, responsible being, a concept which is crucial to personal and social integration and development. The benevolent philosophy of the 'parens patriae' process, Platt comments, 'often disguises the fact that the offender is regarded as a "non-person" who is immature, unworldly, and incapable of making effective decisions with regard to his own welfare and future' (Kittrie, 1971, p. 348). Such an approach cannot but operate as a self-fulfilling prophecy.

There are a number of elements in the argument that the professions can operate to disable people. There is the argument that professionalisation mystifies; it makes simple activities look complex and so deters people from tackling them on their own. If people do not feel able to act on their own, but only with professional advice or help, they become dependent. There is the point that most professionals prefer passive clients and this deepens dependency. Again, in some areas the laity are simply expropriated by the professionals; an area of life becomes professionalised - child birth is a good example. Furthermore, as professionals edge into a new field of activity and gradually take it over, so the technology becomes professionalised, only accessible and comprehensible to professionals and often, finally, only legally available to professionals. The collective impact of these processes is to disable people, to destroy both their confidence and their capacity to act autonomously and independently. It is the end product of dependency. This affects both individuals and communities and leads to abdication of responsibility.

Once such abdication takes place, interest, concern and skills atrophy and are lost forever. 'The community' becomes incapable of consuming its own smoke, of coping with its own problems. Law and order becomes the responsibility of the police, old people of 'the welfare', the provision of places for children to play becomes a responsibility of the council - and so on. Such trends lead to the growth of professional groups and services to cope with a range of needs which were previously satisfied through individual or communal action. The development of such groups and services furthers the process of disablement and abdication as the range of needs dependent on individual and communal action narrows.

Those who have written about the disabling effects of the professions have drawn attention to an important point. Clearly professions can, and do, disable as well as enable. What the critics are attacking, however, is a particular kind of professionalism. The process of disablement is not inevitable. It is the product of a particular view of the role and function of professions and professionals - and their clients. Clearly professions can and do enable as well as disable, but enabling depends on an egalitarian philosophy and the sharing of power and knowledge between professional and client. Preservation of the power, prestige and privileges of the professions depends, or seems to depend, on the maintenance of a decent gulf between professionals and clients. Such a gulf is an important element in the disabling situation and it is an inevitable corollary of the paternal model of professional work, where the professional confronts his client from a position of distant superiority rather than equality. Professionals can start from where people are, building on their capacity to help themselves or they can confront those who seek their services with their own professional definition of the problem which substantially ignores the views and capacities of the person seeking help.

Much of the attack on the disabling effects of the professions is built on a stimulating if insubstantial foundation of assertion. That professions can have such effects is an important insight and contributes to our understanding of the implications of professionalisation. The insight needs, however, to be regarded as helping understanding rather than as explaining the social functions of the professions. The important task is distinguishing between enabling and disabling functions and deciding which models of professional work best contribute to individual and social development.

VII LACK OF ACCOUNTABILITY

Central to the contemporary critique of the professions is concern about their accountability, their responsiveness to popular, political, bureaucratic and client influence and authority. The concern exists at various levels. There has been concern and complaint by those who dislike what the professionals are doing or not doing - the new methods they were introducing in the schools; their dislike of committing delinquents to institutions; the way they were acting as rubber stamps to patient demands for abortion, or, on the other hand, were acting in such a way as to refuse legitimate applications; the way they were casually and callously condemning quite acceptable housing for slum clearance because it lacked certain amenities considered vital by middle-class professionals. As they grew in power, and as their influence and decisions impinged more closely on more people's lives, concern as to the basis of professional power and the nature and strength of the controls upon it became more significant. 'Although the government is the main source of employment and remuneration for doctors, teachers and social workers', write Adler and Asquith, 'the doctors' clinical freedom, the teachers' control over what is taught in the schools and how it is taught, and the social workers' decisions about what kind of help, if any, should be given are largely immune from any form of democratic accountability and control' (1979, p. 6).

The autonomy to which professions and would-be professions aspire has its justification partly in the very nature of the work which such occupations undertake. Much of it is difficult if not impossible to supervise adequately. This might be called the reality argument. Secondly, there is the argument that professional work is so esoteric that only other professionals can understand and assess it - the expert argument. As Lord Horder, Royal Physician through five reigns and arch-opponent of the National Health Service in 1946, put it, 'Only the doctor knows what good doctoring is' (Barnard and Lee, 1977, p. 74). A third justification is the argument that in a free society professionals should be autonomous so they cannot be used as instruments of coercion by the state - the argument of principle. How valid are these arguments?

The problem is to balance a necessary freedom for the professional with a sufficient measure of accountability to ensure a responsiveness to social needs and agreed social purposes. While professions may need and merit a measure of autonomy, their claims must be regarded in the light of claims for privilege rather than as assertions of basic rights.

The autonomy of the professions can be examined on the

basis of four criteria - their degree of self government, their measure of freedom in their work, their ability to ignore research findings and to reject or prevent evaluation, and finally the degree of development of appeal and complaints procedures in their field of work.

The degree of self government achieved by professions can be established fairly easily. The medical profession has, of course, secured a substantial measure of self government. Aneurin Bevan accepted this principle at the outset of the National Health Service. 'There is no alternative', he insisted, 'to self government by the medical profession in all matters affecting the conditions of its academic life. It is for the community to provide the apparatus of medicine for the doctor. It is for him to use it freely in accordance with the standards of the profession and the requirements of his oath' ('BMJ', 16 February 1974). More recently the Merrison Committee reasserted this principle proposing that the profession should be regulated by a body with ninety-eight members, eighty-eight of whom should be members of the medical profession (HMSO, 1975, para. 390). That is as near professional self government as one can hope to come in a sinful world.

Neither teachers or social workers have achieved self government. Both are still at the stage of struggling for some kind of registration council to control entry to the profession. Teachers have secured that all new entrants to teaching must be trained, social workers have yet to secure this step on the road to control of entry to the profession as a stage on the longer trail to full professional self government.

What of freedom in work - the second yardstick of autonomy and one which is more easily secured than the explicit right to professional self government? Teachers, as we have seen lack self government, but they do enjoy a substantial measure of freedom in their work. 'Within reasonable limits', a chief education officer told Kogan, 'the headmaster and his staff are free to run the school as they think best' (1973, p. 54). He went on to point out that this does not mean autonomy to do just as they like, but rather freedom within certain broad conventional limits. Control by teachers over what is taught and how it is taught brings, however, a very considerable measure of freedom in work. As regards the value of school governing bodies as a check on professional autonomy, another chief education officer made the point that 'Any head of standing has little difficulty in ensuring that governing bodies are his creatures' (ibid., p. 176).

The William Tyndale case was a fascinating, long-running case study in the accountability of teachers and the measure of freedom they possess in their work. The Auld Report explores the nature and dimensions of the problem. The major difficulty in making teachers accountable for their work was that in crucial areas

> the Authority has no policy:
> (i) as to the standard of attainment at which its primary schools should aim;
> or
> (ii) as to the aims and objectives of the primary education being provided in its schools, save the very general aim of providing the best possible opportunities to be given to the children to acquire the basic skills and social attainments so that at the age of eleven they can transfer to secondary schools equipped to do so;
> or
> (iii) as to the methods of teaching to be adopted in its schools (Auld, 1976, para. 830).

Such a lack of policy, Auld records, is typical of most education authorities. It means there are no standards or criteria on which schools' and teachers' performance can be assessed. Teachers have, therefore, a very large measure of freedom in their work. The Authority's principal weapon for judging whether a school is performing satisfactorily is its inspectorate but 'the Inspectorate has no formal power to determine the way in which the teaching in a school should be conducted' (ibid., para. 829). Because the inspectorate's role is now predominantly to advise rather than to judge the performance of schools and teachers, the ILEA does not provide for regular full inspection of its schools. Inspections take place only where there is 'some special reason' (ibid., para. 51). Other independent standards of performance such as the number of eleven-plus passes belong to the unenlightened days of the past when educationists believed they could and should attempt to test performance.

'It is difficult to talk of assessing the performance of teachers', Gretton and Jackson point out, 'when there is no agreement on what teachers are supposed to be doing' (1976, p. 123). The educationists have sought, explicitly and implicitly, to secure autonomy for teachers on the score of professional development and responsibility. In the face of that plea, democratic institutions have retreated from what clearly is a complex and difficult undertaking. The William Tyndale case showed that no one was willing to take responsibility for the work of teachers. Their freedom - until crisis was blatantly obvious - was very great. The Tyndale case was, of course, the product of a whole series of minor failures of responsibility which were massive in their total implications. But the case shows the fundamental problem of securing teacher accountability in a system where the lines of responsibility and authority are confused and where no one is clear what the relationship between political and professional authority should be.

Social workers too have a significant measure of autonomy. While individual social workers are accountable for their decisions to those above them in the hierarchy of Social Services Departments, and ultimately to the Social Services Committee, this accountability is more apparent than real unless significant departmental resources are at issue. The evidence available on which the recommendations or action of the individual social worker can be judged is the social worker's own reports on the case. Since the social worker is likely to have made up his or her mind on what action is appropriate before writing the report, it is unlikely to form a good basis for an objective review of what has been decided. So accountability may be more apparent than real. In the way they use their time, and how they allocate it to particular clients or groups of clients, social workers have substantial autonomy.

Freedom at work means the brightest jewel in the glittering crown of the medical profession - clinical freedom. The prescribing practices of general practitioners are subject only to the most residual of checks. It is only the GP whose prescribing is positively profligate who excites investigation. As regards hospital doctors, there are no sanctions at all against a specialist who admits patients unnecessarily, prolongs their stay beyond normal lengths, or carries out an excessive number of tests and investigations.

The scandal at Normansfield Hospital is an illustration of the freedom of the medical profession from accountability in its work, of the breakdown - or non existence - of effective management. 'The vocabulary of management - with its emphasis on monitoring and accountability', writes Rudolf Klein, 'is shown to have been empty, incantatory rhetoric devoid of substance' (1978). There was no effective accountability. In the words of 'The Times' leader on the report 'Normansfield was virtually left by the health services to fester, year after year' (22 November 1978).

The consultant psychiatrist was allowed to continue to preside for many years over a regime which was described by the Committee of Inquiry as 'intolerant, abusive and tyrannical' (HMSO, 1978, p. 10). His power was unchallenged because those in a position to take action were 'obsessed with the difficulty of doing so' (ibid., p. 407). These obsessions had their roots in ideas of clinical autonomy - freedom in work. 'Unfortunately', said the Chairman of the Regional Health Authority, 'in the National Health Service at present, we lack the capability of dealing with a consultant whose ittitude is recalcitrant and domineering' ('The Times', 23 November 1978).

The third criterion against which the degree of professional autonomy can be examined is the ability of a profession to ignore research findings and reject or prevent evaluation of its work. Cochrane and others have shown how the medical profession continues to use many treatments which have been shown to confer no tangible benefits on patients and many more the value of which is highly problematic (Culyer, 1976, pp. 54-5). It has also consistently ignored research which shows that for many medical conditions a shorter hospital stay or outpatient treatment is as conducive to speedy recovery as a period of hospitalisation. The ultimate decision, it is asserted, rests with the individual consultant however convincing the research findings and however great the potential savings.

Much of the research on the impact of social work is now recognised to be of dubious value. The questions asked in the past - does social work work? does it change people? - are simply not susceptible to research investigation. Much of the research, however, has been critical, suggesting the marginal impact of supposed social work skills on clients' attitudes and behaviour, or showing little difference between the work of trained and untrained workers. These findings have made little impact on professional self confidence, on demands for expansion, or assertions of the role social workers could play in areas such as mental health.

Underlying this rejection of formal evaluation are two beliefs - that only the individual professional can judge the effectiveness or efficiency of his work in particular situations, and that there is something in all professional work which transcends any kind of objective measurement. It is this that makes all attempts at evaluation dubious and renders evaluation by non-professionals 'illegitimate and intolerable' (Freidson, 1970b, p. 72).

Times may be changing but up till now the professions have managed substantially to avoid the implications of evaluation of their activities.

The more perceptive members of the professions see that such independence is an anachronism. 'Medicine', McKeown writes, 'must be prepared to face the tests which are inescapable in private enterprise and which it is almost unique among public activities in having evaded hitherto. Is our work well done? Is it worth doing? and, Does it pay its way?' (McKeown, 1976, p. 119). But the majority of the medical profession continues to assert that accountability is solely to the individual patient - an ideology which fits very ill with the idea of a national health service.

A logical corollary of the principle of professional freedom in work and the rejection of outside evaluation is inadequate complaints and appeals machinery. The professions' view seems to be that there is no need for such procedures - almost that those using professional services have no right to complain - and the laity have been reluctant to press the matter in the face of such professional egoism. There is no regular or routine review of the competence, or performance, or up-to-dateness of teachers, social workers or general practitioners. There is therefore complete dependence on the complaints of patients or clients to discover if things are not as they should be. At the same time, of course, the ideology of the professions rejects the notion that any client can ever properly assess the standards of professional practice. 'It is curious,' Freidson muses, 'to find such complete dependence on the client when the ideology of professionalism has stressed that no client can ever properly judge professional practice' (1973, p. 53).

If a patient seeks to complain officially about some aspect of his GP's conduct he faces a range of problems. Understanding the procedures is complex. The machinery is often rusty. There is no provision for assistance in presenting the case, while the doctor will receive help from his professional organisations. The area of legitimate complaint is, in fact, extremely narrow - has the doctor transgressed in relation to his Terms of Service. Most patient grievances are therefore excluded. It can easily be the case that there is simply no way a patient can register a formal protest about what has, or has not, been done. The system can work but it is ill-designed for the tasks it has assumed and as Klein puts it 'As a source of information for pinpointing those doctors who are failing to deliver the goods as specified in their contract, the complaints machinery is little better than spinning a roulette wheel' (1973b, p. 138).

The BMA likes the present system and opposes any change but, as Professor Robson argued to the Franks Committee, 'The fact that it commends itself to the doctors does not seem to me any stronger reason for saying it is necessarily the best system than it would be if one said of our criminal justice system that it was the best system because it appealed to the prisoners appearing in the courts' (ibid., p. 96). Defective as it is, complaints machinery exists in the NHS. In education and personal social services there is really no formal complaints system available to the dissatisfied.

Mental Health Review Tribunals exist to review the professional decisions of doctors about the need to continue compulsorily to detain patients. Essentially the Tribunal exists to protect the patient from the powers which the 1959 Mental Health Act bestows on the medical profession. It is a weak and inadequate form of protection. The most important and weighty evidence which the Tribunal receives is from the Responsible Medical Officer - against whose decision the patient is appealing. If the RMO thinks the patient is suffering from mental disorder it is very difficult to prove he is not. And, as Fennell points out, reports from independent psychiatrists usually carry less weight than the report from the RMO since the latter is in closer touch with the patient and is thus deemed better able to form a reliable opinion on his state of mind (Fennell, 1977, p. 211). The panel composed of a legal member, a medical member and a lay member has to make a decision about the correctness of a professional judgment when the main information at its disposal is a report from the professional whose judgment is being challenged. The expert's judgment is bound in this situation to carry great weight in a body which is supposed to act as a counter to professional judgment.

In certain crucial areas of their work there is, in effect, no appeal from the decisions social workers make. If a social worker refuses material help to a family under Section I of the Children and Young Persons Act 1963 there is no appeal to any body outside the Social Services Department. In the Supplementary Benefit system in contrast, there is the well worn path to the Appeal Tribunal over the right to benefit, the level of benefit and the right to discretionary additions.

Even more important, as has been indicated earlier, when a court makes a care order on a child or young person, the social workers decide what this shall mean - detention in a secure establishment or return home under supervision. There is no appeal from this professional-bureaucratic decision. Social workers are directly accountable to no one for a decision which may mean long-term involuntary detention for a child. The justification is that what is at issue is treatment and this is a matter for an informed professional decision. There can, therefore, be no question of accountability to any body or individual not inducted into the sacred mysteries of the professional art.

Another example of the same hostility to complaints procedures for clients, though in this case it is more explicit, is the response of the medical profession to the Select Committee's proposal that the Health Service Commissioner should be able to consider patients' complaints involving clinical judgment. The annual representative meeting of the BMA passed a motion 'totally rejecting the intrusion of the health service commissioner into the field of clinical judgment' ('The Times', 13 July 1978). This meeting went on to pass a motion deploring the use of medical assessors to help the Commissioner in considering cases and agreed that any doctor accepting such an appointment would forfeit the confidence of colleagues.

There has never been any suggestion that the Commissioner or his lay staff would make clinical judgments. What is at issue is whether complaints about treatment, in addition to maladministration, should be open to investigation by the ombudsman. The Health Commissioner has referred in his reports to his need for medical advice when investigating complaints about maladministration and such advice has been readily forthcoming. The Parliamentary Commissioner has investigated complaints with a clinical element from Broadmoor and Rampton, with advice from medically qualified assessors since his inauguration (F. Stacey, 1973, pp. 78-9). Only an unhealthy and irresponsible desire to avoid all evaluation, even by medically qualified colleagues, can lead to opposition to such a longstop form of safeguard for patients. As the Secretary to the Mental Welfare Commission for Scotland, which has considerable experience of reviewing clinical judgments, wrote in a letter to the Select Committee 'If clinical judgment is sound it should bear investigation by those competent to evaluate it' (HMSO, 1977a, p. xiv). There is little doubt, however, that the profession will be strong enough to prevent such an intrusion on medical privacy and successfully to assert the principle that what individual doctors do is beyond complaint or formal evaluation even by their professional peers.

The general conclusion from this examination is that the professions have a substantial degree of autonomy. When this has been attacked professionals have tended to make two responses. First, they have argued that their main accountability is to their individual clients. Second, they have argued that they are accountable to their professional peers. We have dealt with the first defence in the discussion of professional responsibility and the service ideal. The second needs brief further examination. Does colleague/peer group control operate in such a way as to secure accountability to professionally acceptable standards of behaviour - leaving aside the question of whether such professional standards are more generally acceptable? All the evidence suggests that colleague control is a fragile and ineffective instrument. Normally it operates only in cases where gross professional incompetence occurs, or if the criminal law is broken. The profession as an organised body only intervenes in such extreme situations and this can be little help in ensuring general standards. 'The professions', says Dollery, 'take pride in maintaining their own standards but in practice only intervene in cases where a coroner's inquest or a malpractice suit disclose gross professional incompetence or if the criminal law is broken' (1971, p. 9). At Normansfield Hospital, for example, Dr Lawlor's colleagues sought jobs elsewhere rather than continue to work with him and colleague control failed completely to operate (HMSO, 1978b, p. 10). Colleague control, in the USA, Freidson found, was just the same. In the medical group he studied, belief in the freedom of the individual professional meant that all but 'gross and obvious deviance in performance' was tolerated by colleagues (Freidson, 1975, p. 237). His conclusion elsewhere was that professionalism as such, with its stress on confidentiality and professional discretion, was an obstacle to the distribution of information about performance which was a pre-requisite of colleague regulation (Freidson and Rhea, 1965-6, p. 123). Berlant makes the same point - that there are 'components of the [professional] code which prevent the evaluative process necessary for social control' (1975, p. 39). Because professionals do not - or should not - discuss colleagues' work with each other, they lack the knowledge which is a basic requirement for effective colleague control. Another difficulty about colleague control is its introverted nature. The experience of Normansfield suggests a process of colleague self selection. Those who could not tolerate the situation moved on, those who found it not intolerable stayed. There was, therefore, no kind of professionally objective colleague control. The inquiry into Farleigh Hospital made a very similar point when commenting on the uncritical approach of members of the Hospital Management Committee. The Committee concluded that 'the standards by which the hospital was judged were its own internal standards' (HMSO, 1971, p. 42). The medical professionals established a set of implicit standards - which were unsatisfactory by any objective standard - and then succeeded in colonising the HMC and persuading it that such standards were appropriate.

Professional ambivalence - or weakness - on these issues is all too plain. The evidence of the Royal College of General Practitioners to the Royal Commission on the NHS drew attention to the 'unacceptably low standard' (RCGP, 1977, para. 2.11) of medicine practised by some GPs but it went on to uphold doctors' complete clinical freedom from bureaucratic constraints.

Attempts to design mechanisms to increase professional accountability have so far made little impact. This is because they have not been based on any clear view of what such accountability should mean. The belief that professionals should be left to get on with their work guided only by their ethic of service and their sense of professional responsibility is a strong one. But there seems a ground swell of dissatisfaction with the measure of independence which professionals have. Concern is with the principle and the practice of autonomy. At the level of principle there is in circulation the idea that professionals ought to be accountable to the society which supports them and whose resources they use. This is a political belief, the product of ideology, the age of consumerism, the politics of participation, the attempt to extend the principles of democracy from narrow issues of politics to all areas of life. At the level of practice the concern is simpler; it is with what professionals do and how they do it, with the use they make of their freedom. The objection is not simply to the principle of professional autonomy, but to its impact and implications in the area of social welfare.

Current criticism of the professions has been reviewed under seven headings - the charge that the professions have made large claims but their achievements have been limited; the accusation of failures of professional responsibility;

the attack on the claim to political neutrality; the criticism that they have trampled on individual rights; the challenge to the claim of an ideal of service; the alleged disabling effects of professional activity; and finally the charge that they lack any effective accountability. At the heart of the critique is concern about the power of the professions, the way it is used and its impact in society.

5
Towards a policy for the professions

Illich has argued that the history of industrial society falls into two phases. In the first phase, the application of science to age old problems produces a string of successes and a rapidly rising general standard of living. In the second phase, the achievements of science begin to turn sour and the benefits accrue to certain élite groups rather than to the population at large. Illich applies this analysis to a number of specific institutions of industrial society - most notably to the school and the health care industry (1975b, p. 8). He also applies it generally to the professions, arguing that they must now be regarded as an institution of dubious value in modern society.

Whether or not Illich's analysis and conclusions are fully accepted, it is clear that the present and future roles, functions, powers and privileges of the professions are an issue of debate in many industrial countries. From different sides there are assertions that economic and social development mean the professionalisation of society, its deprofessionalisation or its reprofessionalisation. Whatever the trends, the powerful position of the professions in our welfare system and the questions currently being asked about that position make the question of a policy for the professions an important one.

I THE NEED FOR A POLICY FOR THE PROFESSIONS

This section is concerned with why there is a need for a policy for the professions. The argument rests generally on the evidence presented in the first four chapters of this book and in particular on two propositions - that both the present relationship between the professions and society in Britain and the present relationship between professionals and their clients is unsatisfactory.

The present relationship between the professions and society varies from profession to profession according to age, status and the social significance of its work. Professions have grown and been granted rights and privileges in a purely ad hoc manner. There has been no policy and little thought about the appropriate relationship between the professions and the society in which they operate. An assumption of consensus about social ends, and of good faith and concern only for the common good, has meant that there has been no obvious issue for debate.

The area of difficulty in the relationship between the professions and society can be summed up in one word - accountability - but it has many dimensions. The root of the difficulty is that ideas about accountability have not really advanced from the mythical golden age when independent professionals met independent clients without the intrusion of public welfare organisations. In that idyllic situation, accountability was no problem. In large public services the whole situation is more complex. Who, for example, is the client - the individual user of health or personal social services or the education system or the community which acts as broker and picks up the bill? It is a question which there has been no serious attempt to answer.

The professions assert an accountability to clients and their peers which ignores political accountability. In a situation where professions increasingly work in public services in the pursuit of public purposes, such assertions are an anachronism. Accountability to individual clients is only one part of genuine professional responsibility and that can only be adequately achieved through a broader notion of social responsibility. Similarly, professional self regulation as a mechanism for securing accountability is unsatisfactory. No profession has shown anything but the most luke-warm interest in the monitoring and maintaining of the standard of work of its members.

No one would wish to see the professions totally subservient to the will and whims of the state. Equally, the autonomy to which the professions lay claim fits ill with a democratically agreed range of publicly provided and publicly financed social policies. There has to be accommodation between the professions and the state, preserving the professions as independent critics of public policies while at the same time securing their subordination to agreed public policies and purposes.

The second proposition in the argument that there is a need for a policy for the professions is that the relationship between the professions and those who use their services is less than satisfactory. This is not to say that there is consumer dissatisfaction on a significant scale. What survey evidence shows is a relatively high level of satisfaction with general practitioners (Cartwright and Anderson, 1979), with the hospital service (HMSO, 1979), and with contacts with social workers and social services departments (Goldberg and Warburton, 1979). But there are clearly aspects of professional-user relationships which provide grounds for concern.

An important general point is that traditional professional-client relationships have survived and do survive where they are clearly dysfunctional for the attainment of the goals for which the professionals are supposed to be working. The traditional professional-user relationship has been one in which the client or user's role was to hand over the relevant area of his life to the professional and gratefully follow the advice he was given. A more educated population and new understanding of, for example, the determinants of educability, or the nature of health, render such a pattern of relationships unacceptable. So there must be a different attitude by doctors to health, to their own role and to their patients and the same goes for teachers. 'The possibilities of modern medicine', Brown writes, 'cannot be realised without the support of a better educated public which is more sophisticated in health matters. Inevitably this also implies a more critical public and this in turn will imply changes in the relationship between those giving and receiving medical care' (1973, p. 92). A new pattern of relationships is required to achieve the aims of services.

Another unsatisfactory element in professional-client relationships is the lack of responsibility which professions show for the needs and rights of their clients. Examples have been quoted in earlier chapters of professional failures to pursue client interests through political activity and of professionals' use of their independence to create conditions of work which suited their convenience rather than took account of the needs of their clients - conditions which it was then very difficult for clients to challenge.

A third matter for concern is the way in which the skills and interests of certain professionals are ill-adapted to the now accepted needs of the clients for whom they remain responsible. Many groups of clients are ill-served by the professionals responsible for them, but the professionals nevertheless continue to assert their responsibility - for example doctors and the mentally handicapped, social workers and the elderly and the physically and mentally handicapped.

Although professionals stress a theoretical accountability to clients and their peers, in fact client views and opinions tend to be belittled or disregarded. Because of acute sensitivity about comment on genuinely professional decisions, the professions are reluctant to listen to client views on other aspects of their work, issues on which only the consumer can pronounce. There is little or no acceptance by the professional of the consumer's right to comment on, or to complain about, the substance of the service he is offered or how it is offered.

In this situation the client is left substantially powerless to make known his views or to comment on the service being supplied. What is needed is a professional-client relationship in which discussion and dialogue can take place with mutual respect for what both parties can contribute. Both client and professional lose in the present relationship.

On the basis of this unsatisfactory relationship with society and with clients there is clearly a need for a policy for the professions. It is also possible to see pressures in society making for a change in the position of the professions - the increased questioning of authority and expertise of all kinds, the collapse of economic growth and the obvious high costs of professional services, the growth of a critical consumerism, a search for greater efficiency in welfare, for example.

On the other hand, the professions are part of our kind of society. Their position is what it is because of the nature of our society and because of particular values, patterns of authority and because of a particular social structure. As was argued in Chapter 1, the professions have important 'functions' in a welfare capitalist system such as expressing state concern for particular needs, legitimating particular kinds of state action, providing desirable jobs for the children of the bourgeoisie in a de-industrialising economy, working for the reproduction of labour and the maintenance of social order.

Any change in the position of the professions depends on changes both in professional and popular attitudes and consciousness. The reluctance of those with power and privilege to divest themselves of such burdens is one of the most obvious lessons of history. So too - though less often discussed - is the reluctance of the general populace to assume an active role in the politics of everyday life. People have to change as well as the professionals - to change from seeing themselves as consumers to seeing themselves and acting as exerters and enjoyers of the exertion and the resulting development of their own capacities.

Any general initiative for a new policy for the professions will have to come from government but the links between government and the professions makes such an initiative unlikely. Furthermore, the professions still retain enough of an odour of sanctity for reform-minded governments to be reluctant to incur their wrath and to seem to be coercing groups which have always asserted a respected independence. Governments of the left have a high regard for expertise, governments of the right have enough connections with the more élitist professions to have absorbed a measure of respect for others claiming the same status. Pressures for change are present but the professional position remains a strong one.

II THE PROPER ROLE OF THE PROFESSIONS

There are two central problems in working out a policy for the professions - the first is deciding what the proper role of the professions in society should be, and the second is working out how to make that role a reality. It is these two issues which are the subject matter of this and the following sections. First I explore the question of the proper role of the professions in society.

The first point to be made is that, whatever the utopians and the critics may say, there is no viable current alternative to a professional welfare system. There may be room for a measure of deprofessionalisation in the cracks and crannies of some services, but the real issue is the future shape of professional services and professional relationships. A belief in the continuing importance of the role of the professional makes discussion about the nature of that role all the more important.

Changes in society and in ideas about welfare together with current dissatisfaction about the relationship of the professions with society and with their clients points to one central truth - that professional work needs to be regarded as a partnership. It is a partnership between the professional and the individual client, between the professional and society and between the professional and other professionals.

Partnership means much more than simply a sharing of information though that is clearly crucial. It means, at the end of the day, power sharing - a genuine role for service users in the decision making process about the way the health centre, the school or the social services area office should operate.

This partnership between the professional and the individual also means that the professions must take more seriously what the Webbs described as the most important of all the functions of professional organisations, 'the function of independent, authoritative criticism of the government' (S. and B. Webb, 28 April 1917, p. 48). In the past, the professions have been reluctant to set themselves up as critics of government policies and standards. Professionals have tolerated the intolerable in a way which does their concern for their clients little credit. If professional work means a partnership between professionals and their clients then the professionals must assume, on behalf of their clients, a more critical attitude to government policies which affect the terms and possibilities of that alliance.

Partnership also implies professional acceptance of the validity and value of client comment and assessment of aspects of professional work. There is a sphere where client comment is of little value - how the operation is to be performed, what drugs are best to deal with a given complaint, which method of teaching reading is generally superior, for example - but there are many issues on which only clients know the truth. Their judgments may be subjective but what is real to them is real. Only they can know whether the medicine works, whether the appointments system works, whether surgery opening hours fit with local bus and train times and so on. Only those to be rehoused know how rehousing will affect their lives and whether or not they like the alternative housing which is being offered them. A professional-client partnership means that the professionals accept the legitimacy and value of such feedback as what it is - expert comment.

What does it mean to say that professional work is a partnership between the profession and society? It means recognising the obvious truth that, in the professions and the services with which we are concerned, society as well as the individual is the client. Society finances professional training, sets the objectives of services, and employs and pays the professionals who work in them. The professions cannot avoid their close relationship with the social purposes of the state, but often they seek to avoid the responsibilities which follow - to look at their use of resources in social not just in individual terms, to pursue the implementation of politically agreed priorities which generate little enthusiasm in the profession, to accept the right of management to set boundaries to the limits of professional discretion.

A partnership between the professions and society means clarifying the relationship so that the spheres of legitimate authority are clear. At the moment all sides suffer from the lack of such clarity. For example, describing the weaknesses in the scope for action of a well intentioned health authority, R.G.S. Brown wrote that 'the most important is the persistent failure to find an adequate conceptualisation of the relationship of clinicians to management' (1979, p. 218).

In extreme moments the professions assert the view that politicians have no right to impose decisions upon them. Such a view has no support in theories of representative government. Governments may accept - and perhaps too often have accepted a self denying ordinance when it came to dealing with professionals - or they have retreated tactically in the face of the professional fire power which met their advance - but their right to make the rules cannot be questioned. When, in 1942, the right of the Commons to debate strategy was under criticism Aneurin Bevan vigorously asserted that right. All MPs, he insisted, were present 'as amateurs, not as experts'. Representative government itself, was government of the experts by the amateurs and always had been. 'It is the obligation of this House', he insisted, 'to discuss major strategy, and for hon. Members to say otherwise means that they are undermining the very foundations of representative government' (Foot, 1975, p. 387).

Such vigorous insistence on the right of the laity to control the professionals is rare but important. Politicians have been more apt to allow professional encroachment and to accommodate political power to professional power than to assert and defend the sphere of politics as opposed to the authority of respected, but sectional, interests.

Certain principles of a partnership can be stated. Policy making and the choice of priorities is a political task. Decisions about what should be done and in what order are clearly political - whether services for the elderly should have priority over services for children, for example. How things are to be done is much more an issue for professional advice - for example on how the living conditions of the elderly could best be improved - but the decision remains political. Professional advice is the advice of interested parties and needs to be balanced by other interested advice. Decisions about the organisation of services - health, education or personal social services - are again matters for politicians. They have no special expertise - but neither do the professionals - and given the distributive and re-distributive implications of such decisions they are clearly political rather than professional.

Judgments about need are also political, the stuff of democratic politics. 'The crucial question at the heart of the politics of the National Health Service', writes Culyer,

> is who should be making these judgments? Certainly not the author (an economist), or social scientists in general, or the medics; for while there does exist a school of thought that, because 'experts'' opinions about the facts, the history, the technology, etc., involve both expertise _and_ judgment, their moral judgments also have some special authority. Nothing could be more dangerous than this view to democracy in general in a technical age of large organisations, and nothing could be more alien to the idea of the NHS (1976, p. 145).

Judgments about what constitutes a social need are political, but equally clearly judgments about individual need within the context of public services are professional - the need for a hospital bed or residential care within politically agreed guidelines and priorities. Governments determine priorities, guidelines and standards, the professionals decide how they shall be applied in individual situations on the basis of their expertise.

The third element in the professional role which needs emphasis is that it implies partnership with other professionals. Many professionals can no longer achieve their objectives unless they work closely with other professionals in the same or different services. In relation to providing a satisfactory standard of residential care, for example, the Committee of Inquiry into South Ockendon Hospital argued that the achievement of a homely way of life in mental handicap hospitals depended on a group of individual professionals - doctors, nurses, teachers, occupational therapists, social workers - submerging their individual identities in pursuit of a common goal (HMSO, 1974, para. 598 et seq.). Individual professional objectives could only in fact be achieved through such self immolation. Titmuss has argued the same point. 'The solo entrepreneurial clinical or case-work role', he suggests, 'is no longer adequate by itself in many cases: someone has to enable (or to mobilize) a variety of services and agencies to come into play in the interests of the total needs of the individual and his or her family' (1968, p. 74).

Delivering effective services to some groups has been made more difficult by what Peter Self has styled 'the Balkanisation of public programmes and policies' (1972, p. 293). Such professional organisation accords ill with many of the needs of clients. The only way to avoid the ill effects of such forms of organisation is to emphasise the notion that professional work in many cases must involve partnership with other professionals as an essential element.

It is important to emphasise the tripartite nature of the professional partnership which is being suggested as a new basis for professional work because that has a crucial balancing effect. The partnership with society which could lead to the total subordination of a profession to public purposes is balanced by the profession's partnership with individuals, so the profession does not become the slave of government. Similarly, stress on the partnership of a profession with other professions can be a check on the professional partnership with individual clients.

The professions are both the servants of society and the servants of individuals. They can only succeed in their work if the dual nature of the responsibility is welcomed and if the basis of the relationship is accepted as one of partnership. Stress on societal and individual partnership leads naturally to a greater emphasis on the importance of partnership with other professionals.

Professional partnership is put forward as the appropriate role for professionals in society for two reasons - because a relationship of partnership is seen to be the best starting point for successful professional work and because such a relationship is seen as the appropriate one in a democratic society. Clearly the precise nature of the partnership will need to be worked out separately for different occupations and different services. What is important is to assert the principle.

III REFORMISM AND A NEW RELATIONSHIP

The traditional mechanism for securing the desired position of the professions in society is political. Democratically elected councillors and members of parliament ensure, in theory, that all areas of government policy are compatible with the wishes and needs of the population, that serious grievances can be aired and that special interests are subordinated to general social purposes. But as Nevil Johnson has argued, this does not provide the kind of accountability the service user needs. It is 'too blunt an instrument as well as one which blurs the real problems by expressions of censure rather than a search for adjustment of the complex institutions involved in the changing of priorities and needs' (1974, p. 7).

In some areas of social welfare there is considerable machinery for dealing with user grievances and for representing consumer opinion. In other areas there is virtually a complete absence of such institutions. In health the machinery is elaborate and complex - if ineffective - both for representing consumer views and for hearing complaints. In the personal social services, in spite of the views expressed by the Seebohm Committee about the crucial importance of citizen participation in the running of personal social services (HMSO, 1968b, para. 49 et seq.), there is no machinery by which users of services may make their views known or by which they can formally appeal against discretionary decisions by members of staff. In education, parent-teacher associations and parental representation on school governing bodies gives parents a notional voice in school development. On the other hand, in some Local Education Authorities there is no effective system of local appeal if parents are dissatisfied with the school to which their children have been allocated - and the national appeal system can take months to activate.

Dissatisfaction with simple political accountability has led to various experiments designed to secure more direct accountability of professionals to society and to consumers. There has been the attempt in town planning at mass participation of those affected by potential planning decisions. In health and education there has been what might be styled representative participation - in Community Health Councils, and in parent and community representation on school governing bodies. These experiments in representative participation of service users can be divided into participation without power, as in CHCs which only possess the power to report and comment without any share in management, and participation with at least notional power as in, for example, the new powers given to school governors in Sheffield in recent years. These initiatives show some of the difficulties in devising new representative institutions of this kind.

Any organisation which is purely representative and has no opportunity to implement its ideas or ensure that they are implemented is, when the chips are down, weak. The CHC may be able to bark - at times loudly enough for even the bureaucrats and the professionals to incline an ear - but it has no bite. CHCs also live with a continuing anxiety about the legitimacy of what they say. Who do they represent? In what sense can they be said to speak for the public? How can they find out what people think about the health issues of the day? Should the CHC set out to be statesmanlike - a sort of shadow Area or District Authority - or should it take a terrier role - snapping at the heels of an apprehensive Health Authority, chasing it first one way and then another according to the public concerns of the moment? These problems need not prevent a CHC from doing useful work but they do raise continuing questions about the legitimacy of what it does and says. It can be a useful place in which informed and committed individuals, often speaking for particular interest groups, can bring pressure to bear on the health authority, but it cannot hope to represent the views of the total community - because the community may well have no views at this general level of concern and because the Council has no means of finding out what such views are if they do exist.

Another difficulty which faces the Councils is that they do not have direct contact with service providers. Their direct links are with management. This is the correct link for the discussion of general issues of policy, but for many issues direct contact with general practitioners or consultants would be more helpful. The Council does not provide a forum for direct discussions between users and service providers.

An interesting experiment in the representation of consumer views in education is the attempt in Sheffield since 1969 to reform and revitalise school governing bodies with parent representatives, teacher representatives, representatives of industry, trade unions, parish councillors and others including pupil representatives in secondary schools. The governors are 'to have general direction of the conduct and curriculum of the school' - representative participation with power. Did this lead to changes? The answer seems to be that it did not. The governors showed little willingness to invade what they saw as the professional territory of the teachers. 'A large proportion of board members', Bacon comments, 'are professional people who have, in the main, learnt to accept that one must fully respect the competence and professional integrity of one's fellow workers, lest they in turn question your own authority' (Mack, 1978; cf. Bacon, 1976, 1978a and b).

The end result of the new democratic, participative system may well, Bacon argues, increase the authority of the head teacher in the school and community because his policies and decisions gain the added authority and legitimacy granted by the seal of democratic, community and consumer approval. As Baron and Howell pointed out some years ago, 'without initiative from the Head, a governing body can do little to become an effective partner' (1968, p. 99).

Various methods of representing consumer views to professionals and service managers have been used in social services with results which can hardly be called encouraging. Clearly building consumer representation into services is not simple. There is difficulty in grafting representative institutions on to undemocratic, managerial structures as with Consumer Health Councils. Equally, mass participation of those immediately affected by a policy - as in planning - can be more productive of conflict than partnership. Even when participation is introduced at the level of the school, traditional patterns of lay deference can mean that little changes. In a society based on ideas of representative rather than participative democracy this is unsurprising. If experience teaches scepticism and caution, that is all to the good. Clearly there has to be hard thought about the units, issues and areas for participation and how it is to be introduced - how professionals and consumers are to be prepared for a new relationship.

Another approach aimed simply at narrowing the scope of professional power and reasserting power of another kind is to re-emphasise the role of law as a proven instrument both for securing the rights of individuals aggrieved by the treatment they have received from individuals or institutions, and for securing the subordination of professionals to public purposes. Certainly in the United States the scope of judicial business has broadened immensely in the last two decades. 'The result', says Horowitz, 'has been involvement of courts in decisions that would earlier have been thought unfit for adjudication. Judicial activity has extended to welfare administration, prison administration and mental hospital administration, to education policy and employment policy ...' (1977, p. 4). The Gault case 'rang in the new regime of juvenile law' (ibid., p. 171) and asserted the legal rights of juveniles against the 'unbridled discretion, however benevolently motivated' (ibid., p. 174) possessed by the juvenile court. It asserted the role of law against the power of the professional.

Bean has suggested that one answer to the great power of the professionals in the mental health field would be to provide the patient with more legal rights, such as the right of appeal to an independent tribunal or to a court prior to admission. 'This would mean', he writes, 'resurrecting the machinery of the 1890 Lunacy Act, but without an independent hearing I fear the abuses will continue' (1978). Judges and lawyers are, however, also professionals. As such they are schooled to accept the judgments of other professionals as being made on the basis of expertise and the needs of the client. Since the passing of the 1959 Mental Health Act, Jones points out, judges have shown 'a marked reluctance' to challenge the expertise of psychiatrists and 'they appear to see their role as that of helping the professionals protect society from the irrational acts of deviants rather than protecting the rights of those deviants' (R. Jones, 1978).

The use of law as a means of regulating user-professional relations can also be profoundly destructive. The vast growth of malpractice suits against American doctors has led to an enormous increase in the costs of medical care because of the insurance premiums doctors have to pay, and has led to a pattern of defensive medicine which leads doctors to practise bearing in mind all the time the need to cover themselves against the possibility of the accusation in the future that they did not undertake all possible tests and procedures. Law has a part of play in ensuring continued professional competence and accountability but it should be a weapon of last resort rather than an instrument for regular use.

Another historic, if not nostalgic, approach to creating a new and different relationship for the professions with society and with individual clients is to try to reactivate a market situation with healthy competition between professionals which would put a premium on sensitivity to consumer wishes and destroy the power given by monopoly. It would also remove any problem of the relationship of the professionals to society because society as such would not be involved. The transaction would be simply between professional and client. The issue of subordination to social purposes is disposed of easily and painlessly.

McKie's approach to the problem of urban renewal is one of general reliance on market pressures. He would like the demand for renewal to be related not to professional decisions about the fitness or unfitness of housing but to effective demand expressed through the market. When no one wants particular houses then they are clearly obsolete and should be cleared - but not before then. McKie makes the same plea too in relation to the standards to be set for new dwellings arguing that they 'must be related to effective demand in both the public and private sectors rather than to long term predictions about future requirements made by architects, town planners and other "experts" with scant regard for present cost'. In this way the professionals become accountable and take on their legitimate role. 'Planners working in urban renewal must be prepared to operate through the motives and preferences of occupiers and developers rather than against them: to be highly skilled technical managers rather than paternalistic ideologists' (McKie, 1971, p. 62). What McKie is seeking is a situation in which consumer preferences carry the weight which they carry in a true market situation. The market stands as a model - or myth - of ideal, free egalitarian relationships, - an ideal which could, in fact, be realised in public services more easily than in the free market.

A more idiosyncratic approach to forging a new relationship between professional and client is Roth's stress on the importance of 'the right to quit' as a way of enhancing client freedom. 'Even more important,' he continues, 'is its effect in giving a person a crucial bargaining element in his relationship with authorities, superiors, experts. The very fact that it is known to others that he can quit a relationship will keep in check any tendency to abuse their power over him and will increase the likelihood that they will listen to his demands and be willing to compromise with them' (Roth, 1973, pp. 395-6). This assumes that the person quitting one doctor, for example, can find another who will see him - which is not always the case in some areas in the National Health Service. Again, there may not be another accessible school for a child to go to. The principle, however, is a useful one and could be used in a pure or modified form. Freidson, for example, suggests that patients should periodically have to re-subscribe or re-contract or formally vote 'Yes' or 'No' in a confidence vote in regard to particular local medical services (1970a, p. 225). Recognition of such a principle could make a reality of free choice of doctor in the NHS. A periodic renewal of contract would give users more power than a recognition of a rather abstract 'right to quit'.

A further way in which the balance of power in relationships between professionals and their clients can be altered in medicine in particular is by greater emphasis on the principle of informed consent as a condition of the conduct of medical procedures. Roth says there can be no doubt that this principle - particularly in the USA - 'is having a major impact on professional-client relationships in medical care' (1977, p. 201).

One way of combating the power and influence of particular groups is, of course, to create or institutionalise sources of countervailing power. Peter Self has argued that civil servants should have a much deeper knowledge of particular policy fields (1972). Their dependence on the advice of experts would thus be lessened since they would be better able to evaluate professional claims. They, and their political masters, would then be less likely to be colonised by the professionals and to accept their views as final statements of objective truth. It has also been argued as an extension of this 'information brings power' argument that a more professional system of political control could also reduce professional power. As long as councillors are part time, and poorly recompensed for their work, they will be unable to match the expertise or the arguments of the professionals.

These proposals for the investigation of new methods to increase accountability through political change, the use of law, a reassertion of market principles, a redefinition of professional-client relationships and the deliberate construction of sources of countervailing power, would operate at the level of day-to-day professional work. The issue can also be approached from a different level. Klein has suggested on a number of occasions the need for a body such as a Select Committee for the Professions (1974b, p. 38), a Permanent Council on the Professions (1973b, p. 160), and a Standing Committee on the Professions (1975, p. 339). His idea is for a body with appropriate staff which would regularly collect and publish information about complaints procedures, procedures for monitoring standards of work and for ensuring continued competence, and about how the various professional councils, corporations and associations were exercising their powers and responsibilities. Such a body could have an extremely important role in securing greater professional accountability. It could subject professional bodies and practices to the kind of critical and informed questioning which they too easily escape at the moment. It could also be an important influence and watchdog in a movement to create institutions to secure greater accountability - new representative institutions, new complaints procedures and so on. It could carry out a regular review of each major social welfare profession - of, for example, its government, training and education, level of staffing, adaptation to new needs, acceptance of research findings, its efficiency and effectiveness, its relationship with government, with its clients and with other professions.

The proposals considered in this section all have something to offer but they fall short of a genuine policy. Rather they represent a kind of guerrilla warfare against the professions rather than an attempt to establish a new relationship based on new principles. By the nature of the problem there can be no slick institutional solutions. A policy cannot be formulated and then deftly implemented by a few swift turns of the legislative machine. The professions have to be persuaded of the force of the argument that current relationships with clients are both a factor in unsatisfying work and dysfunctional to the achievement of the goals they are pursuing. They have to be persuaded of the real advantages of a partnership relationship for them and for their clients. Professionals have also to be persuaded to re-examine the nature of their relationship with society with the aim of creating a more satisfying partnership. Similarly, clients, if they are to use professional services effectively, must be liberated from a passive consumer approach to their role in relationships with professionals and see themselves as partners. None of these changes are going to happen quickly. What is important is to be clear about the relationship which is sought and with how it can be furthered and to seek to move in the desired direction.

How should government be proceeding in the present situation to move towards a new partnership relationship for the profession? A number of things can and should be done straight away.

There is certainly a strong case for the establishment of a body on the lines suggested by Klein. A Select Committee could provide a satisfactory mechanism for a continuing critical scrutiny of professional practices and for the encouragement of innovations leading to new relationships. A body such as a Select Committee would also root the issue firmly in the political field - which is where it belongs. If government is to develop a policy for the professions there is clearly a need for some kind of public or parliamentary body to oversee such a policy.

Basic to the new policy would be the encouragement and development of ad hoc representative institutions. It is at the level of service delivery that users are most involved in the service, and have most to contribute to its improvement. So the new partnership requires local institutions - for the Health Centre, the group practice, the school, the Social Services Department Area Office - Patients' Committees, governing bodies, management committees - where the professionals and user representatives can discuss the functioning of the organisation within the broad framework of policy laid down by government. Ingrained attitudes of deference by service users and of paternalist authority from professionals are going to inhibit the effective functioning of such bodies - and they will not vanish overnight - but there is a basis for a new relationship in the needs of both sides. Users need to voice their views and anxieties about appointments systems and emergency cover, about new methods and approaches in school, about the implications of professional-inspired welfare policies for the neighbourhood. The professionals have an equal need to speak about, for example, when and when not to call a doctor, about what doctors can and cannot do, about the possibilities of new educational methods and the problems of school discipline in a changing and permissive society, about why some juvenile offenders seem to get off while others are sent away. All professions need public support for their work and this means public education at a local level, which means new institutions.

The idea that professional work is essentially a partnership with the resulting implication of tripartite accountability also carries with it implications for the resolution of complaints and differences between professionals and consumers and an acceptance that complaints and differences are to be expected. The need therefore is for appeals and complaints systems which are quick, simple to understand and use and readily accessible. Of the professional welfare services, only the NHS has a formal complaints system. Its various elements have been thoroughly examined in recent years - and found sadly wanting (Klein, 1973b; F. Stacey, 1978; M. Stacey, 1974; HMSO, 1973; HMSO, 1977a). The system is complex and lengthy, it is not designed to take in many of the problems which most worry patients and is weighted against the complainant. The development of local Patients' Committees could provide a forum for the discussion and resolution of issues of this kind so solving one of the problems of the current complaints machinery, but the need for improved machinery remains (I. Shaw, 1978).

The present system of professional-patient relationships is the product of certain values and attitudes which have no place in the partnership model of professional work. The surrounding of medical practice with a protective maze - with the dissatisfied patient challenged to negotiate it - is the product of the professional obsession that no lay person can possibly comment sensibly on medical procedures. Such an attitude has no place in modern medicine. A quick, simple, informal system for dealing with complaints, including complaints about clinical judgment, is a necessary element in all services.

Another important direction in which the idea of a partnership between the professions and society can be developed is through encouragement of political and managerial authority in relation to professionals. Too often political bodies are reluctant to assert their authority. The Committee of Inquiry into Normansfield Hospital roundly condemned the idea that there was nothing the Regional Health Authority could have done about the situation because of doctors' clinical freedom to pursue their own judgment. 'Health Authorities', it concludes, 'have a right, and indeed a duty, to stipulate, if they feel it necessary, the pattern of life that they wish to provide in the hospitals for which they are responsible (this particularly applies to long stay hospitals); and it is equally their duty to take disciplinary action against any employee who deliberately thwarts their intentions.... They should not allow themselves to be confused, still less stopped in their tracks, by the use of such terms as "clinical responsibility"' (HMSO, 1978b, p. 407).

Against professional claims - implicit or explicit - that their obedience is to some higher good and nobler vision, politicians and managers can assert their own obedience to the common good as defined by the democratic will of the people mediated through Parliament or the processes of local government. The Taylor Committee's argument that the social nature of the school justifies lay involvement in all aspects of its life is one which should be taken to heart by all managers in the field of social welfare. 'A school', the Committee pointed out (and they could equally well have said the same of a health service or a personal social service system or a planning department), 'is not an end in itself; it is an institution set up and financed by society to achieve certain objectives which society regards as desirable' (HMSO, 1977b, para. 6.14). That is a complete justification for the assertion of political and management authority. Such ideas need to be expressed clearly and loudly.

Management can and should press the professions to a greater self consciousness about the implications and impact of the decisions they make. It can confront them with a profile of how they use their time, the decisions they make, the resources they use and comparisons with the work of their colleagues and with national norms. Management has both the right and the duty to assert its ability to see situations more broadly than individual professionals and to claim the authority which such a perspective gives.

Professional self audit can contribute to the same professional self consciousness about the resources used and the distributional implications of the decisions made, about the implications of decisions for individuals, about the nature and need for cooperation with other professionals. Professional self audit must be accepted as a corollary of professional responsibility to clients and to society and as a condition of freedom. 'Despite recent developments', said the Royal Commission on the National Health Service, 'we are not convinced that the professions generally regard the introduction of audit or peer review of standards of care and treatment with a proper sense of urgency. We recommend that a planned programme for the introduction of such procedures should be set up for the health professions by their professional bodies and progress monitored by the health departments' (HMSO, 1979, para. 12.56).

There are many models of self audit which might be adopted but the American Professional Standards Review Organisations provide a useful starting point for consideration. The Organisations are controlled by a National Professional Review Council which has certain statutory duties - to establish local norms of diagnosis and treatment, to set up norms for the length of hospital stay and to provide for the review of these for individual patients, to construct 'profiles' of patterns of work for each doctor, institution and patient. The aims are simple - to see that all medical care given is medically necessary, meets appropriate standards of quality, care and duration. In the words of one American commentator 'Doctors are seeking to transform their historic implicit responsibility to ensure good care into an explicit public accounting' (Sanazaro, 1974).

The range and variety of these suggestions suggests both how considerable is the concern about the position of the welfare professions and how considerable is the thought which has been given to modifying that position. Many of the suggestions reviewed here are perceptive and have practical potential. If put into effect, relationships would change. All the evidence, however, is that such changes even if significant here and there would ultimately be marginal. There are severe limits to what can be achieved through sneaky social change - the philosophy of Fabian reformism. Things can be changed - history proves that - but not drastically and the more incisive and radical the proposals, the more likely they are to be strongly resisted.

It may be that in the real world the approaches outlined here are the best we can do. All we should attempt, perhaps, is a little reining in here and a little wing-clipping there. Nevertheless, while we tinker, armed with the tools and oil cans of piecemeal social engineering, we should be aware of the limitations of our approach - and look beyond it.

IV REALISING A NEW RELATIONSHIP

The starting point for any proposals for a radical change in the role and social relationships of the professions must be George Bernard Shaw's comment on how the problematic relationship between society and the medical profession could be altered. 'The social solution of the medical problem', he wrote, 'depends on that large, slowly advancing, pettishly resisted integration of society, generally called Socialism' (1974, p. 67). The argument is a simple one - only through political change of this kind with new values and ideologies and with a new approach to economic, social and political relationships will the professions emerge clearly as public servants working with their clients for mutually agreed ends and purposes. It may be argued that the experience of other countries is unconvincing and that the problem of the proper role of the professions seems to survive even radical political change. That is often true. A new relationship between professions, clients and society is not necessarily forged on the anvil of social revolution. But such radical change in the whole approach to the organisation of economic and social life remains a necessary, if not a sufficient, condition of the kind of partnership advocated in this chapter. Such egalitarian relationships cannot grow and flourish in a society whose pivot is inequality.

The radicals who seek to suggest reforms in central social institutions such as the professions always have to pick an uneasy path between the practicable and their real desires. To seek to explore possible avenues of change is not to ignore their limitations. To realise that radical change in particular social institutions depends on fundamental economic, social and political change should not lead to a neglect of possible methods of ameliorating an existing situation. The radical has to live with the tensions involved in his desire for change now and his realisation that the scope for change is limited when the institutions with which he is concerned are a central element in society.

The radical must work for change in the unsatisfactory here and now as well as for the attainment of the end state at which he aims. The basis for such an effort in relation to the professions is not a mystic faith in the benefits of a more democratic, participatory welfare system. It is the conviction that the present position of the professionals is dysfunctional to the operation and development of social welfare policies. A new model of professional relationships based on partnership with society, clients and other professionals is a necessary if not a sufficient condition of the development of a more acceptable, efficient and effective social welfare system.

Bibliography

Abel, R.L. (1979), The Rise of Professionalism, 'British Journal of Law and Society', vol. 6.

Abel Smith, B. (1975), 'A History of the Nursing Profession', Heinemann.

Abel Smith, B. (1976), 'Value for Money in Health Services', Heinemann.

Adler, M. and Asquith, S. (1979), Discretion and Power, paper prepared for SSRC Workshop on Discretionary Decision Making, Edinburgh.

Auld, R. (1976), 'William Tyndale Junior and Infant Schools Public Inquiry: A Report to the Inner London Education Authority', ILEA.

Bacon, A.W. (1976), Parent Power and Professional Control - A Case Study in the Engineering of Client Consent, 'Sociological Review', vol. 24, no. 3.

Bacon, A.W. (1977), Co-management and the School System - a Case Study of Teacher Representation on School Governing and Managing Bodies, 'Educational Studies', vol. 3.

Bacon, A.W. (1978a), 'Public Accountability and the Schooling System', Harper & Row.

Bacon, A.W. (1978b), Democratic Values and the Managerial Prerogative: a Case Study of Head-teachers and Democratised School Boards, 'Educational Studies', vol. 4, no. 1.

Banting, K.G. (1979), 'Poverty, Politics and Policy', Macmillan.

Barnard, K. and Lee, K. (eds) (1977), 'Conflict in the National Health Service', Croom Helm.

Baron, G. and Howell, D.A. (1968), 'School Management and Government' (Research Studies for the Royal Commission on Local Government in England, no. 6), HMSO.

Bayley, M. (1973), 'Mental Handicap and Community Care', Routledge & Kegan Paul.

Bean, P. (1975), The Mental Health Act 1959 - Some Issues Concerning Rule Enforcement, 'British Journal of Law and Society', vol. 2.

Bean, P. (1976), 'Rehabilitation and Deviance', Routledge & Kegan Paul.

Bean, P. (1978), Are the Mental Health Guardians Abusing Their Powers?, 'The Times', 3 January.

Bean, P. (1979), The Mental Health Act 1959: Rethinking an Old Problem, 'British Journal of Law and Society', vol. 6.

Bean, P. (1980), 'Compulsory Admissions to Mental Hospitals', Wiley.

Becker, H.S. (1971), 'Sociological Work', Allen Lane, Penguin.

Bell, D. (1974), 'The Coming of Post Industrial Society', Heinemann.

Berger, P. (1977), 'Pyramids of Sacrifice', Penguin.

Berlant, J.L. (1975), 'Profession and Monopoly: A Study of Medicine in the United States and Great Britain', University of California Press.

Bledstein, B.J. (1976), 'The Culture of Professionalism', Norton.

Bosanquet, N. (1978), 'A Future for Old Age', Temple Smith.

Bottoms, A.E. (1974), On the Decriminalization of English Juvenile Courts, in R. Hood (ed.), 'Crime, Criminology and Public Policy', Heinemann.

Bradshaw, J.R. (1978), 'Doctors on Trial', Paddington.

British Association of Social Workers (1977), 'Mental Health Crisis Services - A New Philosophy'.

Brown, R.G.S. (1973), 'The Changing National Health Service', Routledge & Kegan Paul.

Brown, R.G.S. et al. (1975), 'New Bottles: Old Wine', Institute for Health Studies, University of Hull.

Brown, R.G.S. (1979), 'Reorganising the National Health Service', Blackwell and Martin Robertson.

Butler, J.R. et al. (1973), 'Family Doctors and Public Policy', Routledge & Kegan Paul.

Byrne, E.M. (1974), 'Planning and Educational Inequality', National Foundation for Educational Research.

Carlson, R.J. (1975), 'The End of Medicine', Wiley.

Carr-Saunders, A.M. and Wilson P.A. (1933), 'The Professions', Oxford University Press.

Cartwright, A. and Anderson, R. (1979), 'Patients and Their Doctors 1977', Institute for Social Studies in Medical Care.
Coates, R.D. (1972), 'Teachers Unions and Interest Group Politics', Cambridge University Press.
Cochrane, A.L. (1972), 'Effectiveness and Efficiency', Nuffield Provincial Hospitals Trust.
Cockburn, C. (1977), 'The Local State', Pluto.
Cooper, M.H. (1975), 'Rationing Health Care', Croom Helm.
Cox, C. and Mead, A. (1975), 'A Sociology of Medical Practice', Collier-Macmillan.
Cox, W.H. (1976), 'Cities: The Public Dimension', Penguin.
Crossman, R.H.S. (1972), 'A Politician's View of Health Service Planning', University of Glasgow Press.
Crossman, R.H.S. (1976), The Rôle of the Volunteer in Modern Social Service, in A.H. Halsey, 'Traditions of Social Policy', Blackwell.
Crossman, R.H.S. (1977), 'The Diaries of a Cabinet Minister', vol. 3, Hamish Hamilton and Jonathan Cape.
Culyer, A.J. (1975), Health: the Social Cost of Doctor's Discretion, 'New Society', 27 February.
Culyer, A.J. (1976), 'Need and the National Health Service', Martin Robertson.
Culyer, A.J. and Cullis, J.G. (1975), Hospital Waiting Lists and the Supply and Demand of Inpatient Care, 'Social and Economic Administration', vol. 9.
Cruikshank, K. and McManus, C. (1976), Getting into Medicine, 'New Society', 15 January.
Danbury, H. (1976), Mental Health Compulsory Admissions - the Social Worker's Viewpoint, 'Social Work Today', 10 June.
Daniels, A.K. (1973), How Free Should Professions Be?, in E. Freidson (ed.), 'The Professions and Their Prospects', Sage.
Daniels, A.K. (1975a), Professionalism in Formal Organisations, in J.B. McKinley (ed.), 'Processing People: Cases in Organisational Behaviour', Holt, Rinehart & Winston.
Daniels, A.K. (1975b), Advisory and Coercive Functions in Psychiatry, 'Sociology of Work and Occupations', vol. 2.
Davies, J.G. (1972), 'The Evangelistic Bureaucrat', Tavistock.
Davis, K.C. (1976), 'Discretionary Justice in Europe and America', University of Illinois.

Dennis, N. (1970), 'People and Planning', Faber.
Dennis, N. (1972), 'Public Participation and Planner's Blight', Faber.
Didrichsen, J. (1979), Why a Social Work Council Won't Work, 'Community Care', 26 July.
Dollery, C.T. (1971), The Quality of Health Care, in G. McLachlan (ed.), 'Challenges for Change', Oxford University Press.
Donnison, D. (1979), Social Policy since Titmuss, 'Journal of Social Policy', vol. 8.
Donnison, D.V. et al. (1975), 'Social Policy and Administration Revisited', Allen & Unwin.
Donnison, J. (1977), 'Midwives and Medical Men', Heinemann.
Duman, D. (1979), The Creation and Diffusion of a Professional Ideology in Nineteenth Century England, 'Sociological Review', vol. 27.
Durkheim, E. (1966), The Social Context of Professionalization, in H.M. Vollmer and D.L. Mills, 'Professionalization', Prentice Hall.
Eckstein, H. (1958), 'The English Health Service', Harvard University Press.
Eckstein, H. (1960), 'Pressure Group Politics', Allen & Unwin.
Edelman, M. (1977), 'Political Language: Words that Succeed and Policies that Fail', Academic Press.
Ehrenreich, B. and English, D. (1979), 'For Her Own Good: 150 Years of Experts' Advice to Women', Pluto.
Elliott, P. (1972), 'The Sociology of the Professions', Macmillan.
Ennis, B.J. (1972), 'Prisons of Psychiatry', Harcourt Brace Jovanovich.
Esland, G. (1976), 'Politics of Work and Occupations', Open University Press.
Etzioni, A. (1969), 'The Semi Professions and Their Organisation', Free Press.
Eversley, D. (1973), 'The Planner in Society', Faber.
Fennell, P.W.H. (1977), The Mental Health Review Tribunal: A Question of Imbalance, 'British Journal of Law and Society', vol. 4, no. 2.
Fitzherbert, K. (1977), 'Child Care Services and the Teacher', Temple Smith.
Flexner, A. (1915), Is Social Work a Profession?, 'Proceedings of the National Conference of Charities and Corrections', Hildman.

Foot, M. (1975), 'Aneurin Bevan 1897-1945', Paladin.
Forder, A. (1974), 'Concepts in Social Administration', Routledge & Kegan Paul.
Foster, P. (1979), The Informal Rationing of Primary Medical Care, 'Journal of Social Policy', vol. 8, pt 4.
Freidson, E. (1970a), 'Professional Dominance', Atherton.
Freidson, E. (1970b), 'Profession of Medicine', Dodd, Mead & Co.
Freidson, E. (ed.) (1973), 'The Professions and their Prospects', Sage.
Freidson, E. (1975), 'Doctoring Together', Elsevier.
Freidson, E. (1977), The Future of Professionalisation, in M. Stacey et al., 'Health and the Division of Labour', Croom Helm.
Freidson, E. and Rhea, B. (1965-6), Knowledge and Judgment in Professional Evaluations, 'Administrative Science Quarterly', vol. 10.
Freire, P. (1972), 'The Pedagogy of the Oppressed', Penguin.
Friedman, M. (1962), 'Capitalism and Freedom', Chicago University Press.
Fuchs, V. (1972), Health Care and the United States Economic System: An Essay in Abnormal Physiology, 'Milbank Memorial Fund Quarterly', vol. 50, pt 1.
Fuchs, V. (1974), 'Who Shall Live', Basic Books.
Galper, J.H. (1975), 'The Politics of the Social Services', Prentice-Hall.
Gartner, A. (1971), 'Para Professionals and their Performance', Praeger.
Gartner, A. and Riessman, F. (1974), 'The Service Society and the Consumer Vanguard', Harper & Row.
Gerstl, J. and Jacobs, G. (eds) (1976), 'Professions for the People', Schenkman.
Gilb, C. (1966), 'Hidden Hierarchies', Harper & Row.
Gill, D.G. and Horrobin, G.W. (1972), Doctors, Patients and the State: Relationships and Decision-Making, 'Sociological Review', vol. 20.
Glennerster, H. (1975), 'Social Service Budgets and Social Policy', Allen & Unwin.
Goldberg, E.M. and Warburton, R.W. (1979), 'Ends and Means in Social Work', Allen & Unwin.
Goode, W.J. (1957), Community within a Community, 'American Sociological Review', vol. 22.
Goode, W.J. (1960), Encroachment, Charlatanism and the Emerging Professions: Psychology, Sociology and Medicine, 'American Sociological Review', vol. 25, no. 6.

Goode, W.J. (1966), 'Professions' and 'Non-Professions', in Vollmer and Mills, op. cit.

Gramsci, A. (1971), 'Prison Notebooks', Lawrence & Wishart.

Greenland, C. (1970), 'Mental Illness and Civil Liberty', Bell.

Greenwood, E. (1965), Attributes of a Profession, in M. Zald (ed.), 'Social Welfare Institutions', Wiley.

Gretton, J. and Jackson, M. (1976), 'William Tyndale', Allen & Unwin.

Hall, P. (1975), The Development of Health Centres, in P. Hall, et al., 1975.

Hall, P. (1976), 'Reforming the Welfare', Heinemann.

Hall, P. et al. (1973), 'The Containment of Urban England', vol. II, Allen & Unwin.

Hall, P. et al. (1975), 'Change, Choice and Conflict in Social Policy', Heinemann.

Hall, R.H. (1968), 'Occupations and the Social Structure', Prentice Hall.

Halmos, P. (1965), 'The Faith of the Counsellors', Constable.

Halmos, P. (1970), 'The Personal Service Society', Constable.

Halmos, P. (1973a), Sociology and the Personal Service Professions, in E. Freidson (ed.), 'The Professions and Their Prospects', Sage.

Halmos, P. (ed.) (1973b), 'Professionalisation and Social Change', Sociological Review Monograph 20, University of Keele.

Halmos, P. (1978), 'The Personal and the Political', Hutchinson.

Halsey, A.H. (1972), 'Educational Priority', vol. I, HMSO.

Hamilton, R. (1974), Social Work - an aspiring Profession and its Difficulties, 'British Journal of Social Work', vol. 4.

Handler, J.F. (1973), 'The Coercive Social Worker', Rand McNally.

Hannan, C. (1975), 'Parents and Mentally Handicapped Children', Pelican.

Hardcastle, D.A. (1977), Public Regulation of Social Work, 'Social Work', vol. 22, no. 1.

Hargreaves, D.H. (1967), 'Social Relations in a Secondary School', Routledge & Kegan Paul.

Haug, M.R. (1973), Deprofessionalization: an alternative Hypothesis for the Future, in P. Halmos (ed.), 'Professionalisation and Social Change', University of Keele.

Haug, M.R. (1975), The De-professionalization of Everyone, 'Sociological Focus', vol. 8, no. 3.
Haug, M. and Sussman, M.B. (1969-70), Professional Autonomy and the Revolt of the Client, 'Social Problems', vol. 17, no. 2.
Hayek, F.A. (1963), 'The Constitution of Liberty', Routledge & Kegan Paul.
Heidenheimer, A.J. (1973), The Politics of Public Education, Health and Welfare in the USA and Western Europe: How Growth and Reform Potentials have Differed, 'British Journal of Political Science', vol. 3, pt 3.
Heller, T. (1978), 'Restructuring the Health Service', Croom Helm.
Hill, M. (1976), 'The State, Administration and the Individual', Fontana.
Hill, M. and Laing, P. (1979), 'Social Work and Money', Allen & Unwin.
HMSO (1957), 'Report of the Royal Commission on the Law Relating to Mental Illness and Mental Deficiency 1954-7', Cmnd 169.
HMSO (1960), 'Report of the Committee on Children and Young Persons', Cmnd 1191.
HMSO (1961), 'Report of the Interdepartmental Committee on the Business of the Criminal Courts', Cmnd 1289.
HMSO (1967), 'Children and their primary schools', vol. I.
HMSO (1968a), 'The Administrative Structure of the Medical and Related Services in England and Wales'.
HMSO (1968b), 'Report of the Committee on Local Authority and Allied Personal Social Services', Cmnd 3703.
HMSO (1969a), 'Report of the Committee of Inquiry into Allegations of Ill Treatment of Patients and other Irregularities at the Ely Hospital, Cardiff', Cmnd 3975.
HMSO (1969b), 'Report of the Royal Commission on Local Government in England, 1966-9', Cmnd 4040.
HMSO (1971), 'Report of the Farleigh Hospital Committee of Inquiry', Cmnd 4557.
HMSO (1972), 'Report of the Committee of Inquiry into Whittingham Hospital', Cmnd 4861.
HMSO (1973), 'Report of the Committee on Hospital Complaints Procedure'.
HMSO (1974), 'Report of the Committee of Inquiry into South Ockenden Hospital', HC 124.
HMSO (1975), 'Report of the Committee of Inquiry into the Regulation of the Medical Profession', Cmnd 6018.
HMSO (1976), 'Priorities for Health and Personal Social Services in England'.

HMSO (1977a), 'First Report from the Select Committee on the Parliamentary Commissioner for Administration', HC 45 (British Medical Association Memorandum).
HMSO (1977b), 'A New Partnership for Our Schools'.
HMSO (1978a), 'Review of the Mental Health Act 1959', Cmnd 7320.
HMSO (1978b), 'Report of the Committee of Inquiry into Normansfield Hospital', Cmnd 7357.
HMSO (1978c), 'Social Service Teams: The Practitioner's View'.
HMSO (1979), 'Report of the Royal Commission on the National Health Service', Cmnd 7615.
Hoggett, B. (1976), 'Mental Health', Sweet & Maxwell.
Holme, A. and Maizels, J. (1978), 'Social Workers and Volunteers', Allen & Unwin.
Horowitz, D.L. (1977), 'The Courts and Social Policy', Brookings.
Horowitz, I.L. and Liebowitz, M. (1967-8), Towards a Redefinition of the Relation Between Sociology and Politics, 'Social Problems', vol. 15, no. 3.
Horrobin, D.F. (1978), 'Medical Hubris', Churchill Livingstone.
Hughes, E.C. (1958), 'Men and Their Work', Free Press.
Hughes, E.C. (1963), Professions, 'Daedalus', vol. 12.
Hughes, E.C. (1971), 'The Sociological Eye', Aldine.
Illich, I. (1973a), 'Deschooling Society', Penguin.
Illich, I. (1973b), The Professions as a Form of Imperialism, 'New Society', 13 September.
Illich, I. (1975a), 'Medical Nemesis', Boyars.
Illich, I. (1975b), 'Tools for Conviviality', Fontana.
Illich, I. (1978), 'The Right to Useful Unemployment', Boyars.
Illich, I. et al. (1977), 'Disabling Professions', Boyars.
Jackson, J.A. (1970), 'Professions and Professionalization', Cambridge University Press.
Jackson, M.P. and Valencia, B.M. (1979), 'Financial Aid Through Social Work', Routledge & Kegan Paul.
Jaehnig, W. (1979), 'A Family Service for the Mentally Handicapped', Fabian Society.
Jaques, E. (ed.) (1978), 'Health Services', Heinemann.
Johnson, N. (1974), Defining Accountability, 'Public Administration Bulletin', no. 17.
Johnson, T.J. (1972), 'Professions and Power', Macmillan.
Johnson, T. (1977), The Professions in the Class Structure, in R. Scase (ed.), 'Industrial Society-Class Cleavage and Control', Allen & Unwin.

Jones, K. (1977), The Wrong Target in Mental Health, 'New Society', 3 March.

Jones, R. (1978), The Mental Health Act in Court, 'Social Work Today', 28 February.

Jordan, B. (1976), 'Freedom and the Welfare State', Routledge & Kegan Paul.

Katz, A.H. and Bender, E.I. (1976), 'The Strength in Us', Franklin Watts.

King, M. (1968), Science and the Professional Dilemma, in J. Gould (ed.), 'Penguin Social Sciences Survey 1968', Penguin.

Kittrie, N. (1971), 'The Right to be Different', Johns Hopkins University Press.

Klein, R. (1971), Accountability in the National Health Service, 'Political Quarterly', vol. 42.

Klein, R. (1973a), National Health Service: after Reorganisation, 'Political Quarterly', vol. 44, no. 3.

Klein, R. (1973b), 'Complaints Against Doctors', Knight.

Klein, R. (1974a), Policy Problems and Policy Perceptions In the National Health Service, 'Policy and Politics', vol. 2.

Klein, R. (1974b), The Doctors' Dilemma for Accountability, 'Public Administration Bulletin', no. 17.

Klein, R. (1974c), Policy Making in the National Health Service, 'Political Studies', vol. 22.

Klein, R. (1975), The Profession of Medicine, 'Political Quarterly', vol. 46.

Klein, R. (1976a), A Policy for Change, 'British Medical Journal', 7 February.

Klein, R. (1976b), Power, Democracy and the NHS, 'British Medical Journal', 29 May.

Klein, R. (1978), Normansfield: Vacuum of Management in the NHS, 'British Medical Journal', 23-30 December.

Klein, R. (n.d.), 'Notes Towards a Theory of Patient Involvement', Centre for Studies in Social Policy.

Klein, R. and Lewis, J. (1976), 'The Politics of Consumer Representation', Centre for Studies in Social Policy.

Kogan, M. (1975), 'Educational Policy Making', Allen & Unwin.

Kogan, M. and van der Eyken, W. (1973), 'County Hall', Penguin.

Kronus, C.L. (1976), The Evolution of Occupational Power, 'Sociology of Work and Occupations', vol. 3.

Kunitz, S.J. (1974-5), Professionalism and Social Control in the Progressive Era: the Case of the Flexner Report, 'Social Problems', vol. 22.

Land, H. (1978), Who Cares For the Family, 'Journal of Social Policy', vol. 7, pt 3.

Lane, R.E. (1966), The Decline of Politics and Ideology in a Knowledgeable Society, 'American Sociological Review', vol. 31, no. 5.

Larkin, G.V. (1978), Medical Dominance and Control: Radiographers in the Division of Labour, 'Sociological Review', vol. 26.

Larson, M.S. (1977), 'The Rise of Professionalism', University of California Press.

Laski, H.J. (1931), 'The Limitations of the Expert', Fabian Society.

Lee, R.H. (1975), Medical Rehabilitation: Policy Making in the English Health Service, 'Social Science and Medicine', vol. 9

Lees, D.S. (1966), 'Economic Consequences of the Professions', Institute of Economic Affairs.

Levitt, R. (1976), 'The Reorganised National Health Service', Croom Helm.

Lieberman, J.K. (1970), 'The Tyranny of the Experts', Walker.

Mack, J. (1978), What's the Point of Strong School Governors?, 'New Society', 7 September.

Mackenzie, W.J.M. (1979), 'Power and Responsibility in Health Care', Oxford University Press.

Macpherson, C.B. (1977), 'The Life and Times of Liberal Democracy', Oxford University Press.

McKay, D.H. and Cox, A.W. (9179), 'The Politics of Urban Change', Croom Helm.

McKie, R. (1971), 'Housing and the Whitehall Bulldozer', Institute of Economic Affairs.

McKeown, T. (1976), 'The Role of Medicine', Nuffield Provincial Hospitals Trust.

McKeown, T. and McLachlan, G. (1971), A Sociological Approach to the History of Medicine, in G. McLachlan and T. McKeown (eds), 'Medical History and Medical Care', Oxford University Press.

McKinlay, J.B. (1973), On the Professional Regulation of Change, in P. Halmos (ed.) 'Professionalisation and Social Change', Sociological Review Monograph 20, University of Keele.

Mandell, B.R. (1973), 'Where are the Children?', Heath.

Manzer, R.A. (1970), 'Teachers and Politics', Manchester University Press.

Marshall, T.H. (1963), 'Sociology at the Cross Roads', Heinemann.

Maxwell, R. (1975), 'Health Care: the Growing Dilemma', McKinsey.

Mellor, J.R. (1977), 'Urban Sociology in an Urbanized Society', Routledge & Kegan Paul.

Miliband, R. (1977), 'Marxism and Politics', Oxford University Press.

Millerson, G. (1964), 'The Qualifying Associations: A Study in Professionalisation', Routledge & Kegan Paul.

Moore, W.E. (1969), 'The Professions: Roles and Rules', Russell Sage.

Morris, A. (1978), 'Juvenile Justice', Heinemann.

National Development Group for the Mentally Handicapped (1978), 'Helping Mentally Handicapped People in Hospital', Department of Health and Social Security.

Navarro, V. (1978), 'Class Struggle, the State and Medicine', Martin Robertson.

O'Connor, J. (1973), 'The Fiscal Crisis of the State', St Martins Press.

Owen, D. (1976), 'In Sickness and in Health', Quartet.

Pahl, R.E. (1970), 'Whose City? And Other Essays on Sociology and Planning', Longman.

Parker, H. (ed.) (1979), 'Social Work and the Courts', Arnold.

Parkin, F. (1974), Strategies of Social Closure in Class Formation, in F. Parkin (ed.), 'The Social Analysis of Class Structure', Tavistock.

Parry, N. and J. (1974), The Teachers and Professionalism: the Failure of an Occupational Strategy, in M. Flude and J. Ahier (eds), 'Educability, Schools and Ideology', Croom Helm.

Parry, N. and J. (1977), Social Closure and Collective Mobility, in R. Scase (ed.), 'Industrial Society - Class, Cleavage and Control', Allen & Unwin.

Parry, N., Rustin, M. and Satyamurti, C. (eds) (1979), 'Social Work, Welfare and the State', Arnold.

Parsloe, P. (1976), Social Work and the Justice Model, 'British Journal of Social Work', vol. 6, no. 1.

Parsloe, P. (1978), 'Juvenile Justice in Britain and the United States', Routledge & Kegan Paul.

Parsons, T. (1949), 'The Structure of Social Action', Free Press.

Parsons, T. (1954), 'Essays in Sociological Theory', Free Press.

Parsons, T. (1967), 'The Social System', Routledge & Kegan Paul.

Pearson, G. (1975), 'The Deviant Imagination', Macmillan.
Perry, F.G. (1979), 'Reports for Criminal Courts', Owen Wells.
Pinker, R.A. (1971), 'Social Theory and Social Policy', Heinemann.
Power, M.J. et al. (1967), Delinquent Schools, 'New Society', 19 October.
Powles, J. (1973), On the Limitations of Modern Medicine, 'Science, Medicine and Man', vol. 1, no. 1.
Rea Price, J. (1978), Children - and their Act - in Trouble, in M. Brown and S. Baldwin, 'The Year Book of Social Policy in Britain 1977', Routledge & Kegan Paul.
Rees, S. (1978), 'Social Work Face to Face', Arnold.
Reiff, R. (1974), The Control of Knowledge: the Power of the Helping Professions, 'Journal of Applied Behavioural Science', vol. 10.
Reynolds, D. et al. (1976), Schools Do Make a Difference, 'New Society', 27 July.
Robinson, T. (1978), 'In Worlds Apart', Bedford Square Press.
Robson, J. (1973), The NHS Company Inc.? The Social Consequences of the Professional Dominance in The National Health Service, 'International Journal of Health Services', vol. 3.
Roth, J.A. (1973), The Right to Quit, 'Sociological Review', vol. 21, no. 3.
Roth, J.A. (1974), Professionalism - the Sociologist's Decoy, 'Sociology of Work and Occupations', vol. 1, no. 1.
Roth, J.A. (1977), A Yank in the NHS, in A. Davis and G. Horrobin, 'Medical Encounters', Croom Helm.
Royal College of General Practitioners (RCGP) (1977), Evidence to the Royal Commission on the NHS, 'Journal of The Royal College of General Practitioners', vol. 27, April.
Royal College of Psychiatrists (RCP) (1979), 'Report of the Special Committee of Council on the White Paper on the Mental Health Act'.
Rutter, M. et al. (1979), 'Fifteen Thousand Hours', Open Books.
Sanazaro, P.J. (1974), Medical Audit: Experience in the USA, 'British Medical Journal', 16 February.
Schumacher, E.F. (1974), 'Small is Beautiful', Sphere.
Scott, R.A. (1969), 'The Making of Blind Men', Sage.
Scott, R.A. (1970), The Construction of Conceptions of

Stigma by Professional Experts, in J.D. Douglas (ed.), 'Deviance and Respectability', Basic Books.

Scull, A.T. (1975), From Madness to Mental Illness, 'European Journal of Sociology', vol. 16, no. 2.

Self, P. (1972), 'Administrative Theories and Politics', Allen & Unwin.

Shaw, G.B. (1947), 'The Doctor's Dilemma', Constable.

Shaw, I. (1978), 'Patient Participation in General Practice', Welsh Consumer Council.

Simmie, J.M. (1974), 'Citizens in Conflict', Hutchinson.

Sinfield, A. (1969), 'Which Way for Social Work', Fabian Society.

Smith, G. (1977), The Place of 'Professional Ideology' in the Analysis of Social Policy: Some Theoretical Conclusions from a Pilot Study of the Children's Panels, 'Sociological Review', vol. 25.

Stacey, F. (1973), 'A New Bill of Rights for Britain', David & Charles.

Stacey, F. (1978), 'Ombudsmen Compared', Clarendon Press.

Stacey, M. (1974), Consumer Complaints Procedures in the British National Health Service, 'Social Science and Medicine', vol. 8.

Stimson, G. and Webb, B. (1975), 'Going to see the Doctor', Routledge & Kegan Paul.

Strong, P. (1977), Medical Errands: A Discussion of Routine Patient Work, in A. Davis and G. Horrobin, 'Medical Encounters', Croom Helm.

Tether, P. (1979), 'A Development Agency for the National Health Service', Institute for Health Studies, University of Hull (cf. 'New Society', 22 November 1979).

Titmuss, R.M. (1963), 'Essays on the Welfare State', Allen & Unwin.

Titmuss, R.M. (1965), Goals of Today's Welfare State, in P. Anderson and R. Blackburn (eds), 'Towards Socialism', Fontana.

Titmuss, R.M. (1968), 'Commitment to Welfare', Allen & Unwin.

Tolliday, H. (1978), Clinical Autonomy, in E. Jaques (ed.), 'Health Services', Heinemann.

Townsend, P. (1979), Social Policy in Conditions of Scarcity, 'New Society', 10 May.

Townsend, P. (1973), 'The Social Minority', Allen Lane.

Vollmer, H.M. and Mills, D.L. (1966), 'Professionalization', Prentice Hall.

Walker, P. (1979), Tragedy of Darryn Clarke: Blame Must Be Shared by all the Services, 'Community Care', 15 November.
Webb, A. (1975), The Partisans, in P. Hall et al., 'Change Choice and Conflict in Social Policy', Heinemann.
Webb, S. and B. (1917), Special Supplement on Professional Associations, pts 1 and 2, 'New Statesman', 21 and 28 April.
Wilensky, H.L. (1964), The Professionalization of Everyone?, 'American Journal of Sociology', vol. 70, no. 2.
Willcocks, A.J. (1967), 'The Creation of the National Health Service', Routledge & Kegan Paul.
Williamson, J.D. and Danaher, K. (1978), 'Self Care in Health', Croom Helm.
Wootton, B. (1959), 'Social Science and Social Pathology', Allen & Unwin.
Wootton, B. (1959), Daddy Knows Best, 'Twentieth Century'.
Wrong, D.H. (1979), 'Power: Its Forms, Bases and Uses', Blackwell.
'Yale Law Journal' (1954), The American Medical Association: Power, Purpose and Politics in Organized Medicine - The Political Basis of Power, vol. 63, no. 7.
Young, M. and McGeeney, P. (1968), 'Learning Begins at Home', Routledge & Kegan Paul.
Zola, I.K. (1972-3), Medicine as an Institution of Social Control, 'Sociological Review', vol. 20, no. 4.

Index